SAINT BERNARD

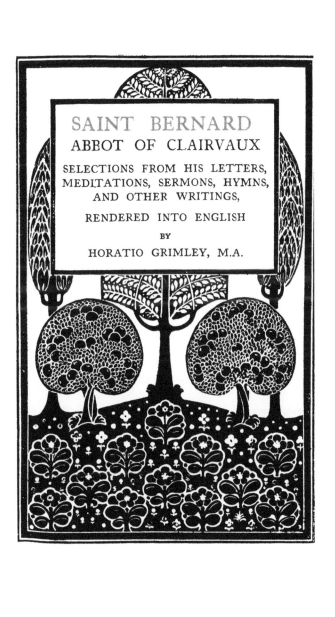

SAINT BERNARD
ABBOT OF CLAIRVAUX

SELECTIONS FROM HIS LETTERS,
MEDITATIONS, SERMONS, HYMNS,
AND OTHER WRITINGS,

RENDERED INTO ENGLISH

BY

HORATIO GRIMLEY, M.A.

CAMBRIDGE UNIVERSITY PRESS
Cambridge, New York, Melbourne, Madrid, Cape Town,
Singapore, São Paulo, Delhi, Mexico City

Cambridge University Press
The Edinburgh Building, Cambridge CB2 8RU, UK

Published in the United States of America by Cambridge University Press, New York

www.cambridge.org
Information on this title: www.cambridge.org/9781107643277

First published 1910
First paperback edition 2013

A catalogue record for this publication is available from the British Library

ISBN 978-1-107-64327-7 Paperback

TO

ALL BY WHOM

IMPRESSIVE UTTERANCES OF THE PAST

ARE RECEIVED WITH WELCOME

GREETING

SAINT BERNARD AND CLAIRVAUX

Bright the valley; but its bright name
From its far brighter Abbot came,
Bright in descent from knightly race
Bright with what cometh from God's grace.
Brightly shone he in eloquence,
Yet with a brightness more intense
He passed through consecrated days
Of mystic thought and prayer and praise.
E'en death robed him with light, not gloom,
And brightness too illumed his tomb.
Now in the light of Love Divine
Greater brightness in him doth shine.

ADAM OF S. VICTOR († 1192).

CONTENTS

		PAGE
	INTRODUCTION	xi
I.	SAINT BERNARD and his Cousin Robert	1
II.	Saint Bernard and Prior Guigues . .	5
III.	Saint Bernard and Count Hugo . .	8
IV.	Saint Bernard and Canon Ogerius .	10
V.	Saint Bernard and Pope Honorius II. .	11
VI.	Saint Bernard and Louis Le Gros .	13
VII.	Saint Bernard and Pope Honorius II. .	16
VIII.	Saint Bernard and Pope Honorius II. .	18
IX.	Saint Bernard and the Bishop of Albano	21
X.	Saint Bernard and William of St Thierry	24
XI.	Saint Bernard and Bishop Alexander of Lincoln	27
XII.	Saint Bernard and Bishop Gilbert of London	31
XIII.	Saint Bernard and Archbishop Hugo of Rouen	33
XIV.	Saint Bernard and Archbishop Hildebert of Tours	35
XV.	Saint Bernard and Archbishop Reginald of Rheims	37
XVI.	Saint Bernard and Master Geoffrey .	39
XVII.	Saint Bernard and King Henry I. .	42

CONTENTS

		PAGE
XVIII.	Saint Bernard and Abbot Richard of Fountains	43
XIX.	Saint Bernard and Duke Conrad of Zeringen	45
XX.	Saint Bernard and the Knights of the Temple	47
XXI.	Saint Bernard and Three Saintly Maidens	57
XXII.	Saint Bernard and the Duke and Duchess of Lorraine . . .	67
XXIII.	Saint Bernard and Pope Innocent II.	69
XXIV.	Saint Bernard and Master Henry Murdach	71
XXV.	Saint Bernard and Prior Thomas of Beverley	73
XXVI.	Saint Bernard and Thomas of St Omer	75
XXVII.	Saint Bernard and Bishop Ardutius of Geneva	77
XXVIII.	Saint Bernard and the Monks of Clairvaux	79
XXIX.	Saint Bernard Preaching to his Monks	86
XXX.	Saint Bernard and the Cistercian Abbots	90
XXXI.	Saint Bernard and his Brother Gerard	92
XXXII.	Saint Bernard and his Brethren at Fountains	109
XXXIII.	Saint Bernard and Abbot Henry Murdach	112
XXXIV.	Saint Bernard and Hugo, a Novice .	114

CONTENTS

PAGE

XXXV.   Saint Bernard and Pope Innocent II.   116
XXXVI.   Saint Bernard and Pope Innocent II.   119
XXXVII.   Saint Bernard and Abbot Baldwin
           of Rieti   123
XXXVIII.   Saint Bernard and King Roger of
           Sicily   126
XXXIX.   Saint Bernard and the Abbot of
           St Aubin   130
XL.   Saint Bernard and Bernard of Pisa .   132
XLI.   Saint Bernard and Pope Innocent II.   135
XLII.   Saint Bernard and the Queen of
           Jerusalem   138
XLIII.   Saint Bernard and King Louis VII.   142
XLIV.   Saint Bernard and the Roman Curia   144
XLV.   Saint Bernard and Pope Eugenius III.   148
XLVI.   Saint Bernard and the French Clergy   154
XLVII.   Saint Bernard and the Abbess Hilde-
           garde   157
XLVIII.   Saint Bernard and Count Hildefons   158
XLIX.   Saint Bernard and Saint Malachi .   159
L.   Saint Bernard and the Duchess of
           Burgundy   172
LI.   Saint Bernard and Pope Eugenius III.   174
LII.   Saint Bernard and Abbot Suger   .   175
LIII.   Saint Bernard and Count Theobald   177
LIV.   Saint Bernard and Pope Eugenius III.   179
LV.   Saint Bernard and the Queen of
           Jerusalem   182
LVI.   Saint Bernard and his Uncle Andrew   185

CONTENTS

		PAGE
LVII.	Saint Bernard's Last Letter	188
LVIII.	Saint Bernard on the Mystery of the Soul	189
LIX.	Saint Bernard and Saint Victor	200
LX.	Saint Bernard on "The Name of Jesus"	203
LXI.	Saint Bernard. Advent Meditations	204
LXII.	Saint Bernard on Loving God	211
LXIII.	Saint Bernard on Consideration	221
LXIV.	Saint Bernard's Hymn in Praise of Jesus	251
LXV.	Saint Bernard's Prayer to Christ upon the Cross	261
LXVI.	Saint Bernard on Worldly Vanity	281
LXVII.	Saint Bernard's Death	285
	INDEX	287

INTRODUCTION

THE sixty-two years of Saint Bernard's life—
from A.D. 1091 to A.D. 1153—have their
earliest and latest decades marked by two memorable enterprises. Bernard's boyish enthusiasm
was doubtless stirred by the First Crusade. For
the Second Crusade he himself kindled enthusiasm
in others.

The names prominent in English history in
Church and State during Bernard's lifetime are
those of St Anselm and Henry I. and Stephen;
while the names of Louis VII. in France and
of Henry V. and Conrad II. and of the Popes
Innocent II. and Eugenius III. (Saint Bernard's
own disciple) may be mentioned in connection
with European continental history.

Saint Bernard was born in the castle of his
father, the knight Tescelin, at Fontaines-les-Dijon.
As the two miles separating the village from the
centre of Dijon are traversed, just before leaving
the Burgundian city the statue of the saint, who
with upraised hand is in the attitude of preaching,
is passed. Before the village is reached, the spire

and tower of the church of St Ambrosien come into view. The hill surmounted by this church would form an appropriate background for an ecclesiastical picture. The atmosphere around seems tinged with religious sentiment.

Within view of the church is the site of Saint Bernard's ancestral castle. Seven children were born to Tescelin and his lady Aletta. Bernard was the third son. His mother's life was a pattern of simplicity, devotion, and charity. Bernard ever tenderly remembered her. Doubtless the remembrance of her ascetic sweetness enabled Bernard so to influence his five brothers as to induce them to adopt the same resolve that he himself had cherished from his earliest days,—the resolve to enter upon a life of thought and devotion within monastic walls. Even his sister, Humbeline, though she long resisted her brother's appeal, later on, with her husband's consent, entered upon a cloistered life.

Bernard himself in his twenty-second year was admitted as a novice in the monastery of Citeaux, by the English Abbot Stephen Harding. Four of his brothers were received at the same time. The fifth and youngest brother also presented himself, but was sent back to remain with his father and sister for another two years. When they had passed by he too was admitted.

At the end of the same two years, Bernard was sent forth from Citeaux with twelve companions to found a new monastery. This he did, in the diocese of Langres, in a valley watered by the river Aube, and called, inasmuch as it was wild and uncultivated, the Valley of Wormwood. The valley soon, under the devoted care of the monks, changed its aspect, and received a new name, Clairvaux, the Valley of Light. By this name it is still known.

Bernard was henceforth known as the Abbot of Clairvaux. His history onwards until the time of his death is so entwined with the history of western Europe as to be almost inseparable from it. He was recognised as the master-mind of Europe, and dignitaries, ecclesiastical and secular, sought and accepted his counsel. The selections in this little book from his many writings confirm and illustrate the statements here made.

I cannot do other than recall that my interest in Saint Bernard was first aroused by a series of week-day evening lectures on his life delivered in a church. I remember too how soon after my own ordination I noticed that whenever I entered the study of a Cornish vicar, a friend of mine, I invariably saw open upon a desk—or perhaps it was upon a large easel—a ponderous volume of the works of the saint, and how I was made aware that from these works my friend constantly gathered materials for impressive sermons. The interest thus aroused and sustained has since been increased by visits—let me call them pilgrimages —to various scenes associated with Saint Bernard's thoughtful toils. His birth-place, Fontaines-les-Dijon, has more than once caused me to arrest my wandering footsteps. Châtillon-sur-Seine, the scene of the saint's school-boy days ; Citeaux, his first monastery ; Clairvaux, founded by himself, and with which his name is so closely associated , Sens, the scene of a memorable encounter with Abelard ; and the valley of the Rhine ;—by visiting these my interest in the saint whose memory I was taught to reverence in younger days has been prolonged and intensified.

The selections translated do not include any that have reference to Abelard. The limits of this book would not have provided sufficient space for the insertion of selections bearing upon the controversy between the Abbot of Clairvaux and the Breton teacher, and such could not well have been introduced without reference to the varied experiences and the calamities of a pathetic career.

On the site of the castle in which Saint Bernard was born there have been built in recent years a mission-house, an oratory, and a church.

On my last visit, two years ago, I found the build-
ings deserted by their former occupants, but left
in charge of a peasant nun. She said that four
years previously the mission-fathers, five in number, had been counselled by the then Bishop of
Dijon, as a measure of prudence, in view of a
recent legislative enactment, to disperse themselves. In obedience to their Bishop this the
mission-fathers of Saint Bernard resolved to do ;
but before they could quit the scene of their
devotions and activities, one of them died from
sorrow of heart. So that my last pilgrimage to
Saint Bernard's birth-place was one of sadness.

HORATIO GRIMLEY.

NORTON RECTORY, SUFFOLK,
Festival of Saint Bernard,
1910.

I. SAINT BERNARD AND HIS COUSIN ROBERT.

[1119 ...... 28.]

Saint Bernard reproacheth his Cousin Robert
for deserting Citeaux for Cluny.

From the world forsooth thou didst come,
Robert, not from Cluny, as thou thyself dost
know. Thou didst seek to be received, thou
didst plead, thou didst storm the very portal ;
but by reason of thy tender age thou wast then
bidden to wait, though thou wast not willing to
do so. And when that interval, endured patiently
and without blame, came to an end, then at last,
thou, by prayers, and, as thou mayst remember,
by many tears, didst obtain a long-looked-for
favour ; and the admission amongst us which
thou didst undoubtedly desire, thou didst secure.
After this, having passed through with complete
patience a year of probation, in accordance with
the rule, having associated with us with consistent
faultlessness, thou wast with thine own free will

G.   I   I

professed. Then didst thou first, having cast
aside secular attire, put on the habit of our
Religion.

O foolish youth, who hath bewitched thee that
thou shouldst not fulfil thy vows, which thy lips
have uttered? Shalt thou out of thine own mouth
be justified, or shalt thou not out of thy mouth be
condemned?

Look into thine own heart, examine thine
intention, take counsel with truth; let thy conscience tell thee, why thou didst depart, why thine
Order, thy brethren, thy position here, and myself
who am both near to thee in blood and nearer to
thee in spirit, thou didst desert. If thou art now
living more strictly, more correctly, more perfectly, be at ease, since thou hast not looked back,
and thou mayst glory with the Apostle, who saith:
"Forgetting those things which are behind, and
reaching forth unto those things which are before,
I press toward the mark for the prize of the high
calling of God in Christ Jesus."

But if it be otherwise, be not high-minded but
fear, since howsoever thou dost indulge thyself, in
food, in superfluous dress, in idle words, in lax
and curious wanderings, further than thou didst
promise and didst observe with ourselves, in such
thou hast, far beyond doubt been looking back,
been a shuffler, hast apostatised. I declare as

2

II. SAINT BERNARD AND PRIOR GUIGUES.

[1125 ...... 34.]

For Guigues, Prior of the Chartreuse, amongst fathers most reverend and amongst friends most dear, and for the other holy men who are with him, Brother Bernard of Clairvaux wisheth eternal salvation.

I have received the letter of your holiness as gladly as I with eagerness had for long desired it. Your salutation glowingly sent forth and glowingly welcomed, was by me received, as I confess, not as though it came from man, but as descending from Him who sent His blessing to Jacob. Blessed by the Lord be ye, who have cared to anticipate me with blessings of such sweetness, that there is given to your humble servant boldness to reply to you who have written first ; that such boldness is given to him who hath for long earnestly desired to write to you, but did not presume to do so. I very much feared

5

to invade, by importunate scribblings, the holy
quietness which ye have in the Lord, and your
constant religious silence away from the world;
or to interrupt even for a while your whispered
communings with God, and to proffer my words
to ears inwardly echoing with praises secret and
from above.

*   *   *

Man at first loveth himself on account of himself alone. He is forsooth fleshly, and he is able
to know nothing except himself. When however
he seeth that he is not able to subsist by himself,
he beginneth by faith to enquire after God and
to love Him as necessary for himself. Thus he
loveth God on a secondary stage, for his own
sake, not for the sake of God. But when he shall
have thus begun, because of his own need, to
worship God and to approach Him in thought,
in reading, in prayer, and by obedience, by a sort
of familiarity, little by little, God gently maketh
Himself known to him, and soon becometh acceptable to him. So having tasted how sweet
the Lord is, he passeth to the third stage and
loveth God not for his own sake but for the sake
of God Himself. On this stage he chiefly abideth,
and I know not if by any man the fourth stage is
in this life perfectly arrived at, so that, forsooth,
a man shall love God only for God's sake. If

6

there be any who say that they have had experience of this, to me, I confess, it seemeth impossible. But without doubt, this will not be when the servant having been good and faithful shall enter into the joy of his Lord, and shall overflow with delight in the treasures of God's house. Then in ecstasy, in a wonderful way, he shall be forgetful of himself, and as if swooning spiritually out of himself, he shall entirely lose himself in God, and henceforth shall be united to Him as one spirit.

III. SAINT BERNARD AND
COUNT HUGO.

[1125 ...... 34.]

To Hugo, Count of Champagne, made a
Knight of the Temple.

If for the cause of God thou hast from being
a count become a mere soldier, and from being
rich hast become poor, I congratulate thee of a
surety, and in thee I glorify God, knowing that
this change is the doing of the right hand of the
Most High. But because thy presence to me,
such a cause of joy, hath been withdrawn by
I know not what decree of God, so that I may not
be able even occasionally to see thee, deprived
of whom I could wish, if it were possible, never
to be, I do not comport myself, I confess, with
quietness of mind. And why? Can I be unmindful of thy friendliness of former days and of the
benefits which thou hast so bountifully conferred
on my house of Clairvaux? May God, for love
of whom thou hast done this, keep thee in His

8

eternal remembrance. For we, as much as in us lieth, henceforward not at all ungrateful, will keep in mind the memory of thine overflowing kindness, and if not hindered will show that we do so by our deeds. O how willingly would we have provided for the needs of thy mind and body and for thy soul too, if it had been allowed unto us to continually dwell together! But since that is not to be, it remaineth that for thee whom we cannot have present with us, we shall, in thine absence from us, ever pray.

IV. SAINT BERNARD AND
CANON OGERIUS.

[1126......35.]

To Ogerius, a Regular Canon.

I applaud thee, also, because thou hast not
sought a new teacher, or a new home, but hast
returned to the cloister in which thou once didst
dwell, to be subject again in all homeliness to the
paternal authority formerly so beneficent to thee.
... And I counsel thee to be simple in thy converse with the brethren, devout towards God,
disposed to hearken to thy teachers, obedient to
thine elders, considerate to thy juniors, gentle in
the sight of the angels, useful in speech, humble
in heart, courteous towards all.

V. SAINT BERNARD AND
POPE HONORIUS II.

[1126 ...... 35.]

To the supreme Pontiff Honorius, a certain brother, by profession a monk, in conversation a sinner, writeth, conscious of his own little worth.

They say that with you of more avail is the prayer of a poor man than the look of a powerful one. Such pious opinion of your singular nobleness leadeth me to dare without any fear to write to your Holiness, especially when charity also suggesteth that I should do so. It is of the Church of Chalons, my Lord, that I speak ; as to which Church, I cannot refrain, nor ought I to refrain, from declaring to my utmost its danger. We who are nigh see too clearly how very speedily the peace of the memorable Church will be gravely disturbed, if to the election of that illustrious man, that is, of Master Alberic—to which election both clergy and people with one vote and one voice have in every way agreed—it should be impossible to obtain the assent of your Holiness. As to which if my opinion is desired or is cared for, I know Alberic as a man who hath stood forth hitherto conspicuously as of sound faith and doctrine ; who hath been prudent both in divine and in human things ; and I hope that in the House of God (if He should make choice of him) he will be a vessel of honour, and will be useful not only to that House, but also to the whole Gallican Church. It is for you in your discernment now to judge, whether is worthily solicited from you the bestowal of a dispensation from which such excellent results can be hoped for.

VI. SAINT BERNARD AND LOUIS LE GROS.

[1127 ...... 36.]

To Louis, the glorious King of France, Stephen,
Abbot of Citeaux, and the whole assembly
of the Cistercian Abbots and brethren, wish
health, good fortune, and peace in Jesus
Christ.

The King of heaven and earth hath given you
a kingdom on earth, and will give you also one in
heaven, if that which you have received you shall
zealously endeavour to administer justly and
wisely. What we desire for you, and pray for
you is this, that here you may reign faithfully,
and there blissfully. But with what intent do
you resist so keenly these same prayers of ours
for you—prayers which, if you bear in mind, you
so humbly asked for? For with what sort of
hopefulness are we to presume to lift up our
hands for you to the Spouse of the Church, whom
you thus, and, as we think, without cause and

13

with thoughtless daring, make sad? A grave
lament indeed against you she placeth before her
Spouse and Lord, while him she had accepted as
a defender, she hath to endure as an antagonist.
Do you now consider against whom you make
yourself thus offensive? Against the Bishop of
Paris? No! but against the Lord of Paradise.

This is what we have a care to press upon
you, boldly indeed yet lovingly. We advise and
pray you by that mutual friendship of ours, and
by that brotherhood with which you with due
dignity allied yourself, but now do so severely
injure, that you speedily separate yourself from
such great wrong-doing.

Otherwise if we are not deemed worthy of
being heard, but are slighted—we, your brethren
and friends, and who daily pray for yourself and
your children, and your kingdom—from this ye
shall now know that our littleness to the full
extent of what it can do, is not likely to fail to
render service to the Church of God, and to her
minister, forsooth, our venerable father and friend,
the Bishop of Paris, who, soliciting our humble-
ness against you, hath requested by the right of
brotherhood letters from ourselves in his support
to the Lord Pope. But we, deeming it just,
first by this letter to approach your Excellency,
especially because the same Bishop, by the hand

14

of all the Religious, pledgeth himself to be submissive to justice, if only first of all—which indeed justice itself seemeth to demand—his possessions, unjustly taken from him, be restored.

In the meanwhile we defer forwarding the petition, and wait. And if indeed by God inspiring you it shall please you to incline an ear to our prayers, and, in accordance with our counsel and desire, to re-enter upon peace with the Bishop, yea rather with God, we are prepared for the sake of this matter, to take even a wearying journey to you, wheresoever it shall please you ; but if not, it is necessary that we should hearken to our friend, and show forth our obedience to the priest of God. Farewell.

VII. SAINT BERNARD AND
POPE HONORIUS II.

[1127 ...... 36.]

For the supreme Pontiff Honorius, the Abbots of
the poor of Christ, Hugo of Pontigny, and
Bernard of Clairvaux, desire whatever the
prayers of sinners can avail.

The tearful complaint of the Bishops, yea
rather of the whole Church, we who also are her
sons, are not able to hide. Of what we have seen
we speak. A great necessity hath indeed drawn
us from our cloisters into public life, where also
what we have seen we speak of. We have seen
sad things and of sad things we speak. The
honour of the Church in the time of Honorius
hath been not a little wounded. The humility,
say, rather, the constancy, of the Bishops had
already bent the king's wrath, when, lo ! from the
supreme Pontiff supreme authority intervening,
hath, alas! cast down constancy, set up pride.
We know indeed that from you must have been

gotten, by falsehood—as from your letter is plainly to be gathered—the mandate in which you have ordered to be set aside so just and so necessary an interdict. But whether the falsehood should not at length be seized upon, shall not injustice feel that it hath lied to itself, and by no means to such great majesty as yours? But what we marvel at is this, with what reason an enquiry should have been made with a view to one party only, and that a decision should have been issued against the absent. Which indeed we complain of, not with rash presumption, but with filial love. We suggest to the paternal heart, how greatly from this both the impious one is uplifted with pride and the poor vexed. How long he ought to suffer, or to what extent you ought to suffer with him, it is not for us to prescribe to you. As to this, rather, most tender Father, take counsel with your own heart. Farewell.

VIII. SAINT BERNARD AND POPE HONORIUS II.

[1127 ...... 36.]

*To the same Pope, in the name of Geoffrey, Bishop
of Chartres. He explaineth to the Pontiff
how it was that the Bishop of Paris was
unjustly oppressed by King Louis, who, compelled by the interdict from the Bishops of
France, had promised restitution, but had
been made more contumacious by the absolu-
tion obtained from Honorius, and so had not
made the restitution.*

Superfluous it is to unfold again to you the
sequence and cause of a most sad history. I do
not reiterate the matters which, when the good
Bishop of Paris wrote to you, must have indeed
stirred your fatherly heart. Yet for a brother
and fellow Bishop my testimony ought not to be
wanting. What I have seen and heard I have
considered it necessary to make known briefly.

When the complaints of the before-named

18

Bishop, made with so much moderation, had been received, all the Bishops of the Diocese of Sens, together with our venerable Metropolitan—certain other religious persons being also associated with us—addressed ourselves to the King, humbly, as we ought, upon the grave injustice rendered to us. We prayed that he would restore to the Bishop, who in no wise had deserved such treatment, his possessions which he had taken from him. We accomplished nothing. Feeling at last that we were deciding to flee to the arms of the Church, he was in fear, and consented that all things should be restored. But, by chance, in the same hour, your letter intervening in which you directed that his country should be set free from interdict, he, lucklessly strengthened in evil, did not at all carry out the good that he had promised. Nevertheless, on the day appointed, as he had again promised to do what was right, we presenting ourselves in his presence, endeavoured to secure peace, and it came not. We sought what was good, and lo! turbulence. This, in effect, hath been done by your letter, that what was maliciously taken away is being with more malice retained, and the things that remain are being every day randomly seized, so much indeed the more securely as he may with the more impunity retain them. The just (as we think) interdict of the Bishop having forsooth been raised by your command, and as our decree which we had prepared, and by which we had hoped to secure justice, hath been suspended out of a shrinking deference to you, we are made in the meanwhile a reproach to our neighbours. How long shall this be? The compassion of your piety will look to it.

IX. SAINT BERNARD AND THE BISHOP OF ALBANO.

[1127 ...... 36.]

To Matthew, Bishop of Albano, Papal Legate to
preside over the Council of Troyes, in 1128.
Saint Bernard excuseth himself in that though
called to aid in certain matters, he had not
responded.

In truth my heart was ready to obey ; but not
with it also, my body. Burnt by the heat of
a fierce and raging fever, and exhausted by
sweats, my weak flesh was not able to act along
with my willing spirit. I desired to go, but the
hindrance I have spoken of stood in the way of
my will, eager though it was for a forward flight.
Whether this be truly so, let our friends judge,
who shutting out every excuse, strive daily,
looking on me as enclosed in the network of
obedience, to withdraw me from the cloister into
cities ; and let them at the same time note that
this hindrance is not one that I have untruthfully

devised, but one that hath presented itself in
grievous fashion: that thus they may find that
there is no counsel contrary to the counsel of God.
Let them either bear a grudge against, or accept
quietly, the divine ruling, by which it happeneth
that though I am willing, I have not the strength
to set forth.

But they say, the cause was great and the
necessity grave. Therefore someone must be
sought for who is skilled in arriving at a decision
as to questions of great import. If they think
I am such a one, I not only think, but I know,
that I am in no way such. Moreover, whether
they are great, or whether they are small, these
matters to which they so press me, I have no
reason to interfere in them. I ask: Are the
questions easy or difficult which you are so eager
to impose on your friend to disturb the peaceful-
ness so kind to him? If easy, they can be decided
without me ; if difficult, they cannot be settled by
me. Unless perchance I am esteemed as one for
whom great and impossible things must be reserved, as though I were able to do what no other
one can. Yet if it be so, O Lord my God, how
are Thy designs frustrated in me alone? Why
dost Thou put under a bushel the light which
could shine forth upon a candlestick? Or, that
I may speak more openly, Why hast Thou made

me a monk, and hidden me in Thy tabernacle, in the day of evil, if I am a man necessary to the world, a man without whom bishops are not able to carry on their work? But this also mine acquaintances have provided for me, that now I seem to speak with unbecoming disquietude to a man of whom I am never wont to think of in my heart unless with serene composure and with every delight. But ye know (to you I say it, my father) that I am always so readily prepared, without any disturbing feeling, that I can keep your commands. It will however be a sign of your indulgence to spare me, whenever you shall discern that I ought to be spared.

X. SAINT BERNARD AND WILLIAM OF ST THIERRY.

[1127 ...... 36.]

From the Apologia to William of St Thierry.

And that I may speak openly, doth avarice do all this, which is the service of idols? If you ask, How? I wonder, How! With such a certain art is money scattered, that it is multiplied. It is expended that it may be increased, and profusion produceth further abundance. Indeed by the very sight of sumptuous but wonderful vanities, men are incited more to give offerings than to pray. Thus riches are drawn from riches; thus money attracteth money; because—I know not how it is—where there is a very ample display of riches, there offerings are made the more gladly. By gold eyes are made to feast on hidden relics, and purses are opened. The beautiful picture of some holy man or woman is made a show of, and the more richly it is coloured, the more holy it is deemed to be. Men rush to kiss it. They are

induced to present gifts. They admire its beauty
rather than venerate its sacredness. Then also
there are placed in a church, not coronals, but
wheels, all jewelled, surrounded with lights, but
not the less refulgent themselves with inlaid gems.
We see too instead of candelabra certain tall
trees, weighty with brass, fashioned with the
marvellous labour of the artificer, and not more
gleaming with the lamps placed upon them, than
with their own jewels. What, thinkest thou, is
sought in these things? The contrition of penitence, or the admiration of onlookers? O ! vanity
of vanities ! but not more vain than foolish. The
Church hath resplendent walls, and yet hath not
the poor. It hath its stones clad with gold, and
leaveth its sons unclad. At the cost of the needy
it gratifieth the eyes of the wealthy. The curious
find that which delighteth them, but the poor find
nothing with which life can be supported. Why
at least do we not treat with reverence the images
of the saints, with which the very pavement
trodden under foot everywhere aboundeth? Often
there is spitting into an angel's mouth : often the
face of a saint is bruised by the heels of those who
walk over it. If you do not spare the sacred
figures, why do you not spare the beautiful colours ?
Why decorate what is soon to be defiled ? Why
colour that which of necessity must be trodden

under foot? Of what use are the lovely forms, there where they are continually stained with dust? What service at least do such things render to the poor, to monks, to spiritual men? We indeed suffer things to be done in a church, which are both hurtful to the vain and the avaricious, and devoid of use for the simple and devout.

Again, what good doth that ridiculous monstrosity do to the brothers reading in the cloister? that deformed beauty, that beautiful deformity, so wonderful to look at? Why there the filthy apes? Why the monstrous centaurs? Why the half-human figures? Why the spotted tigers? Why the fighting soldiers? Why the horn-blowing hunters? You may see there under one head many bodies, and again on one body many heads. Here is seen on a quadruped the tail of a serpent; there on a fish the head of a quadruped. There a beast, in front like a horse, is dragging behind it the half of a goat. Here a horned creature in the hinder part is a horse. In short, so many things and such a marvellous variety of diverse forms everywhere appeareth, that there would be more diversion to read the marbles than the parchments,—in taking a whole day in admiring them one by one, than in meditating upon the law of God. Alas! if there is not shame at such foolish things, why is there not grief at their costliness?

XI. SAINT BERNARD AND BISHOP ALEXANDER OF LINCOLN.

[1129 ...... 38.]

To the honourable Lord Alexander, by the grace of God Bishop of Lincoln, Bernard, Abbot of Clairvaux, sendeth greetings, and wisheth that he may be more honoured in Christ than in the world.

Your Philip wishing to travel to Jerusalem hath found a short way thither, and hath speedily arrived where he desired to go. He hath traversed in short time this great and wide sea, and having prosperously sailed hath touched now the wished for shore, and hath at length attached himself to the harbour of safety. His feet are now standing in the courts of Jerusalem, and Him, whom he had heard of in Ephrata, having found in the fields amongst the woods, he adoreth in the place where his feet have rested. He hath entered the Holy City, and hath obtained a heritage with them of whom it is deservedly said : " Now ye are no more strangers and foreigners, but fellow-citizens with the saints, and of the household of God." Going in and out amongst them, he is as one of the saints. He himself also maketh his boast with the others, saying : " Our conversation is in the heavens." He hath become therefore not a curious spectator simply, but also a devout dweller and a chosen citizen of Jerusalem, not however of the earthly one, to which Mount Sinai of Arabia is joined, which is in bondage with her children, but of the one that is free, the one that is above and is the Mother of us all.

And this, if you desire to know, is Clairvaux. She is Jerusalem, in union with her who is in the heavens, by entire devotion of soul, by a way of life in harmony therewith, and by a certain fellow-ship of spiritual insight. This shall be, as he promiseth, his rest for ever. He hath chosen her for his dwelling-place, because with her is, though not yet the clear vision, still certainly the expecta-tion of true peace, of that of which in truth is said : " The peace of God which passeth all understanding." But this his blessedness, though he hath received it from above, he desireth yet to welcome with your good pleasure, yea rather he trusteth that he hath done this, knowing that you are not ignorant of the utterance of the wise man,

28

that a wise son is indeed the glory of his Father. He beseecheth therefore your Paternity—we also with him and for him beseech—that you cause for the future whatsoever arising from his prebend he hath set apart for his creditors, to remain unchanged, lest in anything he should be found—which be it far from him—a repudiator of what he oweth, and a shirker of his promise ; so that also the offering of a contrite heart which he presenteth daily, may not be received while any brother hath aught against him.   Furthermore he entreateth that the house which he hath built for his mother on church land, with the ground which he there hath assigned, may be granted to the same mother so long as she shall live.

This as to Philip.

I have thought it right to add for yourself these few remaining words presenting themselves to me, yea rather coming to me by inspiration of God, and to take upon myself to exhort you in charity not to regard the glory of this passing world which seemeth to abide, so as to lose that which really abideth ; not to love your possessions more than yourself, that so you may lose both yourself and your possessions.   Do not while present prosperity is smiling upon you, lose sight of it, lest adversity without end come upon you. Let not temporal joy both hide from you the

29

lasting sorrow which it produceth and also hideth.
Let not death be thought of as far away, so that
it may seize upon you unprepared, and so that
life while expected to be long may not suddenly
desert you when you are lucklessly unaware.

XII. SAINT BERNARD AND BISHOP GILBERT OF LONDON.

[1130 ...... 39.]

To Gilbert, Bishop of London, Universal Doctor.

The rumour of what thou hast done hath gone out very far, and hath given out a great odour of sweetness to whomsoever it hath been able to reach. Avarice hath no existence. To whom is this not redolent of sweetness? Charity reigneth. To whom tasteth this not sweetly? When all know this, that thou art truly wise, who hath crushed the greatest enemy of wisdom. This certainly is worthy of thy name and of thy priest-hood. It was surely well that thy spiritual philosophy should brightly declare itself by such testimony, that thy brilliant studies should be completed by this ending. That is the true and undoubted wisdom which despiseth filthy lucre and deemeth it to be unworthy for itself to enjoy companionship with the servile devotion to idols. Not a great thing was it for Master Gilbert to be made a bishop, but that a Bishop of London should live as a poor man, that was plainly magnificent. For the sublimity of the dignity could in no wise increase the glory of a name so great, yet the humility of poverty could add to it very much. To bear poverty with an equal mind is the virtue of patience; to seek it voluntarily is worthy of the praise bestowed on wisdom. He is indeed praised and declared admirable who doth not go after gold: but he who also casteth it from him, shall he not be more honoured?

Thou hast dispersed, thou hast given to the poor, money. But what is money in comparison with that righteousness which thou hast exchanged for it? "His righteousness," it is said, "endureth for ever." Is it thus also with money? Profitable and honourable forsooth it is to give that which passeth away in exchange for that which endureth. May it be given to thee ever so to barter, O excellent Master, worthy to be followed with all praise! It remaineth that thy laudable beginning should follow on to a worthy ending. I have gladly received thy benediction, especially as it is united with such great accumulated joy by reason of this thy perfection.

The bearer of this letter, though on account of himself sufficiently worthy of esteem, I yet even desire for mine own sake also to commend to thy Magnificence. He is indeed for his honourableness and devotion most dear to me.

XIII. SAINT BERNARD AND ARCHBISHOP HUGO OF ROUEN.

[1130 ...... 39.]

To Hugo, Archbishop of Rouen.

If malice waxeth mightier day by day, let it not prevail; if it is turbulent, let not its disturbance extend. Marvellous are the risings of the sea, but more marvellous is the Lord in the highest. Supreme mercy hath dealt benignly with thee, thus far, illustrious Father. For by a foreseeing dispensation, thou art not sooner set over the evil than thou art allied with the good, by whose alliance with thee and example thou mayest become good, and thus afterwards mayest be able even amongst the evil to live righteously. And indeed to be good amongst the good hath with it salvation, but to be so amongst the evil, hath also praise. The one is of as much facility as of surety : the other of as much virtue as of difficulty. For its difficulty forsooth is that of touching pitch and not being defiled, of passing through fire without injury, and through darkness without dimness of vision.

It was sufficient for thee amongst the brethren of Cluny to keep thine innocence; but now amongst the dwellers in Rouen thou hast need of patience. "The servant of the Lord must not strive, but rather be patient towards all." And he must not only be patient, and so unwilling to be overcome of evil, but also peaceful, that so he may overcome evil with good. In thy patience possess thy soul: but be likewise peaceful, so that thou mayest possess the souls committed to thee. Be patient because thou art amongst evil men: be peaceful because thou art set over evil men. Let thy charity have zeal, and let thy severity restrain itself at times. Censure should never be remitted; yet it may often be better for it to be intermitted. The vigour of justice should always be fervent, but never of headlong haste. As not everything that pleaseth is lawful, so not everything that is lawful is also free from entanglement. These things thou thyself knowest better than I, and so I press thee not further. I beseech thee to pray for me earnestly, since incessantly I sin.

34

XIV. SAINT BERNARD
AND ARCHBISHOP HILDEBERT
OF TOURS.

[1130 ...... 39.]

*To Hildebert, Archbishop of Tours, who had not
as yet acknowledged the Lord Innocent as
Pope.*

*To the great priest, and in the word of glory
upraised, by the grace of God, to be Archbishop
of Tours, Bernard, called Abbot of Clairvaux,
sendeth his desires that he may walk in the
spirit and ponder upon all things spiritually.*

Lo, Innocent, that anointed of the Lord, hath
been placed for the fall and rising again of many.
They who are of God are willingly in union with
him; but he who is adverse is either of Antichrist
or is Antichrist himself. The abomination is
seen to stand in the holy place, and that he may
obtain possession of it, he doth burn as a fire the
sanctuary of God. He persecuteth Innocent, and
with him all innocence. Innocent, in truth, fleeth
from the face of Leo. He fleeth according to the
precept of the Lord: " If they shall persecute you
in one city, flee into another." He fleeth, and in

this he hath proved himself a man of apostolic mould, since he hath signalised himself as did the Apostle Paul.

And the flight of Innocent is not one in search of ease. He toileth, indeed, but hath honour bestowed on him in the midst of his toils. Exiled from the great city, he is received with welcome by the world. From the ends of the earth, to him as he fleeth, there is a running with nourishing gifts ; although the rage of Gerard of Angoulême hath not ceased. This sinner looketh on and is angered, and yet Innocent is exalted in the sight of kings and beareth a crown of glory. Have not princes everywhere recognised him as the elect of God? The kings of the French, of the English, and of the Spanish, and lastly the king of the Romans, welcome Innocent as Pope, and acknowledge him as the only Bishop of their souls. A threefold cord is not easily broken. The choice of the best, the approved of the many, and what is more efficacious, the witness of a life of goodness, commend Innocent among all, and confirm him as supreme Pontiff.

To which end, Father, your decision is looked for, though it will be late, as rain upon a fleece of wool. Slowness we complain not of, since it savoureth of gravity and keepeth away the note of levity.

XV. SAINT BERNARD
AND ARCHBISHOP REGINALD
OF RHEIMS.

[1130 ...... 39.]

For the Most Reverend Father and Lord, Reginald
by the grace of God, Archbishop of Rheims,
Brother Bernard of Clairvaux desireth health
and whatsoever a sinner's prayers can bring.

Blessed be God who hath deigned that I should
be consoled by the coming of your letter. And
indeed I am able in some way to return letter for
letter: but when shall I be equal to the duty of
paying back to you this favour of yours, by which
I may rightly boast that I by blessings of so great
sweetness have been led on by you, by which
I have been roused by your appeals, and honoured
by your salutations? Certainly I more than any
am as unworthy of the names you apply to me,
as I am little known to you; but the less I am
worthy the more I am grateful. Nevertheless,
while you are thus, you do as befitteth you, since

you are conscious that you have to be a debtor to the wise and to the unwise also.

Forsooth that repute, by the good odour of which you say the excellency of your dignity hath been moved to the appreciation of myself in my lowliness, is indeed dangerous to me, though not lightly pleasing, since from this winding current the enjoyment most desirable and grateful and which hath nothing like to wind, hath proceeded, that by so great a priest of the Most High, I should have been received into favour even before I had deserved to be known to him.

XVI. SAINT BERNARD AND MASTER GEOFFREY.

[1131 ...... 40.]

To Geoffrey (afterwards Archbishop of Bordeaux).

Fragrance in a flower, and sweetness in fruit, are sought for. Attracted, dearest brother, by the fragrance of thy name, which is as ointment poured forth, we desire to know thee by the fruit of thy deeds. For not only ourselves, but God Himself, who needeth no one, but yet at this time desireth thine aid, if thou dost not comport thyself untruly. Glorious for thee it is to be able to be a fellow-worker with God. To be able to be so and not so to be, is a grievous loss. Further, thou hast favour with God and with man, thou hast knowledge, thou hast a spirit of freedom, thou hast speech lively and persuasive and seasoned with salt ; and it behoveth thee, with such great powers, not to be wanting to the Spouse of Christ at so great a crisis, when thou art a friend of the Bridegroom. A friend is

39

indeed proved in days of need. What, canst thou remain still, when thy mother the Church is severely disturbed? Quietness hath had its time, and holy peace hath up till now had its sway freely and gladly. Now is the time to be doing, since they have set aside the law. That creature of the Apocalypse, to whom hath been given a mouth uttering blasphemies, and who is allowed to make war against the saints, sitteth upon the throne of Peter, as a lion ready for his prey. Another creature also hisseth near to thee, as a whelp lurking in secret places. That fiercer one, this craftier one, have met together alike in one place against the Lord and against His anointed. Let us hasten to burst their bonds asunder and to cast away their yoke from us.

We for our parts, along with other servants of God, who are burning with divine fire, have laboured, God helping us, to make one, people and kings, so as to bring to nought the counsel of perverse men, and to overthrow every loftiness that lifteth itself up against the knowledge of God. And not fruitlessly. The kings of Germany, France, England, Scotland, Spain, and Jerusalem, with all their clergy and people, grant their favour and support to the Lord Innocent, as sons to a father, as a body's members to the head, being desirous to keep the unity of the

Spirit in the bond of peace. Moreover the Church rightly receiveth him whose repute is more brilliant, and whose election hath been found to be more genuinely conducted, he obtaining pre-eminence both by the number and by the merit of those who chose him.

But thou, brother, why hast thou hitherto withheld thy support? We know, indeed, that thou as a son of peace canst in no way be induced to be disloyal to unity. But assuredly this sufficeth not, unless thou studiest both to defend it, and to war also with all thy might against the disturbers thereof. And fear thou not any cessation of peace, since with not a small increase of glory shalt thou be requited, if that wild creature near to thee is by thy zeal tamed or made mute, and if the goodness of God snatch from the mouth of the lion (Leo) so great a prize for the Church, the Count of Poitiers.

XVII. SAINT BERNARD AND KING HENRY I.

[1132 ...... 41.]

To the illustrious Henry, King of England,
Bernard, called Abbot of Clairvaux, desiring
that he may faithfully from his earthly king-
dom serve the King of Heaven, and humbly
obey Him.

In your land there is held property which is
my Lord's and yours—property for which He preferred to die rather than to be deprived of. This
I have made arrangements for obtaining possession of, and am sending some of our soldiers,
who, if it doth not displease you, will search for,
recover, and with a strong hand bring it under
control. And these explorers, whom you see
before you, I have sent to carry on this enter-
prise. They will investigate with keenness the
condition of things, and faithfully report on the
same. Render assistance to them as unto
messengers of your Lord, and by your kindness
to them fulfil your feudal duty to Him.

And may He for His own glory, for your
salvation, for the welfare and peace of your
country, lead you onwards in happiness and
honour to a good and peaceful ending of your
earthly life.

XVIII. SAINT BERNARD AND
ABBOT RICHARD OF
FOUNTAINS.

[1132 ...... 41.]

*To Richard, Abbot of Fountains, and his Com-
panions, who from another Order had passed
over to the Cistercian Order.*

What great things we have heard and obtained
knowledge of, and which our two brothers, the
Geoffreys, have made known unto us, how that ye
have become newly aflame with the fire of God,
how from weakness ye have gained strength, how
ye have brought forth flowers of a freshness that
is holy.

The finger of God this is, working mysteriously,
sweetly renewing, wholesomely changing, not indeed making good men of bad, but better men of
good ones. Who will give me the power to pass
over and see this sight so great? For such
advance is not less wonderful or less joyful than

43

conversion. Except that you much more easily find many worldly men converted to good than one even from amongst Religious pass on to something better. The rarest bird on earth is the monk, who from the level which he hath once reached in the religious life riseth even but a little. Hence what ye have done, dearest brothers, as remarkable as salutary, rejoiceth not only us who long to be servants of your sanctity, but also deservedly so the whole city of God : since the more rare it is the more splendid it is also. For it was necessary in the way of forethought to pass beyond the mediocrity very close to defect, and to turn away from the lukewarmness which provoketh God to cast out, but also it thus behoved you to act for conscience sake. For ye know whether indeed it is safe for those who have professed the holy rule to sit and rest on this side of its exalted purity.

I am grieved that by the untoward urgencies of the day, and by the hurrying messenger, I am constrained to trace out my full affection with a pen writing so briefly, and to compress my wide charity within so limited a parchment. But if anything is absent from it, Brother Geoffrey will supply it with the living voice.

XIX. SAINT BERNARD AND DUKE CONRAD OF ZERINGEN.

[1132 ...... 41.]

To Duke Conrad.

All power is from Him of whom the prophet saith : " Thine is the power, Thine is the kingdom, O Lord. Thou art over all nations." Therefore have I thought it well, O illustrious Prince, to counsel your Excellency how much it behoveth thee to yield to Him who taketh even from princes their breath. The Count of Geneva, as we have received from his own mouth, hath offered and still offereth to act with justice with respect to all things which thou sayest thou hast against him. If after this thou dost go on to invade the land of another, to destroy churches, to burn down houses, to drive out the poor, to perpetrate manslaughter, and to shed human blood, there is no doubt that thou wilt stir up against thee the Father of orphans and the just Defender of widows. And certainly with His anger stirred against thee, it will not be of any advantage to thee to make war with so large a multitude animated with such great bravery. For nothing can hinder the omnipotent Lord of Sabaoth from giving victory to whomsoever He willeth, whether they be many or be few.

These things, I, a poor man, moved by the cry of the poor, have ventured to write to your Magnificence, knowing it to be more honourable for thee to consent to the appeals of the humble than to yield to the force of foes, not that I think thine enemy stronger than thou art, but because I know that God the Omnipotent is more powerful, inasmuch as He resisteth the proud, but giveth grace to the humble. I would have approached thy presence, noble Prince, because of this matter, if it had been possible for me to do so. But now, instead of myself, I have taken care to select these of my brethren, if by chance by their prayers and our own, they may obtain from your Highness either a real peace, if such be possible, or certainly an armistice, while it is permitted us to search for the conditions of an enduring peace, conformable to the will of God, to thine own honour, and to the welfare of thy country. Otherwise if thou dost neither accept the just proposal offered, nor have regard to us who offer our entreaties, yea rather heed not God as He warneth thee by us as to thine own welfare, let Him behold and judge. But we know—what we greatly fear as unavoidable—that such great armies cannot easily come into conflict with one another without most severe disaster to either side.

46

XX. SAINT BERNARD AND THE KNIGHTS OF THE TEMPLE.

[1132 ...... 41.]

THE KNIGHTS OF THE TEMPLE.

A new order of knights lately sprung up is heard of on earth, and in that region in which formerly the Light of the World visibly came from on high in fleshly form. A new order of knights, I say, and an order inexperienced in worldly matters—an order which unweariedly engageth in a twofold conflict, warring both against flesh and blood and against spiritual wickedness in high places.

Fearless certainly is the knight, and safe from all surrounding dangers, who, as he clotheth his body with a breast-plate of iron, also hath his soul clad with the breast-plate of faith. Protected by this twofold armour, he assuredly feareth neither devil nor man. But neither doth he dread death, inasmuch as he desireth to die. For what doth he fear, whether living or dying, to whom

47

to live is Christ and to die is gain? He taketh
his stand boldly and gladly for Christ; but more
doth he desire to depart and be with Christ: for
this is better. Fearlessly then advance, ye knights,
and with intrepid souls, drive away the enemies
of the cross of Christ, assured that neither death
nor life shall be able to separate you from the
love of God which is in Christ Jesus, remembering
in every danger the words, "Whether we live or
die we are the Lord's." How arrayed with glory
are they who return from the battle victorious!
How blessed are they who die as martyrs in the
fight! Rejoice, brave athlete, if thou livest and
conquerest in the Lord; but exult and glory
more if thou shalt die and be united to the Lord.
Life indeed is full of joy, and victory full of glory;
but a holy death transcendeth either. For if
blessed are they who die in the Lord are not they
much more blessed who die for the Lord?

And indeed whether we die in bed or in battle,
precious will be without doubt in the sight of the
Lord the death of His saints. But in battle death
is certainly so much more precious as it is the
more glorious. O fearless is the life where the
conscience is pure! O fearless is the life, I say,
in which without dread, death is awaited, yea
rather is both desired with delight and welcomed
with devotion! O knights truly holy and pro-

tected, and free certainly from that twofold danger, by which such order of men is wont to be threatened when the fighting is certainly not for the sake of Christ! For how often thou who engagest in warfare in a spirit of worldliness, dost thou fear lest thou either kill an adversary in the body, but thyself in the soul, or lest thou perchance be slain by him both in body and in soul? According to the disposition of the heart, forsooth, not from the event of the battle, there is meted out either danger or Christian victory. If the cause of the fighting is a good one, the issue of the fight will not be evil. So that the end arrived at will not be judged to be good, if a cause not good and an intention not righteous have preceded. If with the wish to kill another it shall happen that thou thyself art killed, thou wilt die a homicide. But if thou prevailest, and if with the desire of overcoming thine enemy and revenging thyself, thou perchance slayest thine enemy, thou livest a homicide. But it advantageth not, whether dead or living, whether victor or vanquished, to be a manslayer. Unhappy victory, by which thou, overcoming thine enemy, fallest thyself beneath the assault of wrong-doing. And with anger or pride dominating thee thou wilt in vain boast of having conquered thine enemy. He who neither with the desire of avenging himself,

nor with the mad resolve of conquering another,
slayeth his foe, gaineth a true victory. But I
should not call that a good victory, which was
preceded by such desire or resolve. Of two evils
dying in the body is less grievous than dying in
the soul : for not indeed because the body is slain
doth the soul also die ; but the soul which itself
hath sinned, that shall die.

* * *

What then is the end or the fruit of this
worldly warfare—I will however call it malice
rather than warfare—if both the slayer mortally
sinneth and the slain eternally perisheth? Why,
therefore, O knights, this error so stupendous,
this madness so unbearable, at such cost and toil
to fight for no wages indeed but those of either
death or sin? Ye array your horses with silks,
and ye wear swaying cloaks over your corslets ;
ye paint your shields and spears and saddles ;
your bridles and spurs ye adorn with gold and
silver and with gems ; and with such show as
this, with shameful fury and shameless folly ye rush
on to death. Are these things military insignia,
or are they not rather effeminate adornments?
Will the hostile lance perchance be in awe of the
gold, spare the gems, and not be able to pierce the
richly-wrought corslet? Surely ye yourselves have
very often experienced that certain things are

especially necessary to a warrior, that he should forsooth be bold and untiring and watchful as to his own safety, and fleet in his running to and fro, and prompt in striking ; yet ye on the contrary cultivate in feminine fashion long hair which is a burden to the eyes ; ye baffle your footsteps with your long and abundant robes ; your delicate and tender hands ye bury in your ample and flowing sleeves. More than all this, that which more alarmeth the conscience of a soldier, the cause of fighting is slight and frivolous, by which forsooth such warfare, dangerous as it is, is undertaken. Amongst you nothing else bringeth on warfare and arouseth dispute, except either an unreasonable impulse of anger, or a vain desire for glory, or a longing for some sort of earthly possession. For such causes as these, it is not safe either to slay or to be slain.

*   *   *

But the knights of Christ fight safely the battles of their Lord, in no wise bearing either sin from slaying enemies, or the danger of their own destruction. Since indeed death for Christ must be either endured or dealt out to others, it involveth no sin and meriteth abundant glory. Indeed in the one case there is gain for Christ, in the other Christ is gained,—Christ, who surely and willingly accepteth an enemy's death as retribution, and more willingly offereth Himself to the knight for consolation. A soldier of Christ, I say, slayeth with more honour to himself, and dieth with more merit. When he dieth, himself is benefited; when he slayeth, he benefiteth Christ. For not without cause he beareth a sword. He is a minister of God for the punishment of those who do ill, but for the praise of those who do good. When he slayeth a doer of ill, he is not a manslayer, but—so I should say—a slayer of evil, and plainly an avenger of Christ against those who do wrong, and so is accounted a defender of Christians. But when he himself is slain, he is deemed not to have perished, but to have achieved triumph. The death therefore which he inflicteth is gain for Christ; the death which he receiveth is his own gain. In the death of a pagan a Christian is exultant, because Christ is glorified. In the death of a Christian the bounty of the King is shown forth when the soldier is led forth to be rewarded. The just will rejoice over the first, seeing in it the punishment of an evil-doer. At the death of a Christian, men will say "Verily there is a reward for the righteous; doubtless there is a God who judgeth the earth." But not indeed should pagans be slain, if in any way otherwise they may be restrained from attacking and oppressing the faithful. Now however it is better that they should be slain than that the rod of the sinful should rest upon the lot of the righteous, lest the righteous stretch forth their hands unto iniquity.

But now! If it is not right for a Christian to strike at all with the sword, why did the fore-runner of the Saviour tell the soldiers that they should be content with their wages, and not rather bid them refrain from all fighting?

*   *   *

Let me tell briefly of the manners and life of the knights, how they comport themselves whether in warfare or at home; by which it becometh evident how much differ from one another the soldiers of God and the soldiers of the world.

First indeed discipline is not wanting in either direction, and obedience is in no wise despised, since, as Scripture saith, the son of disobedience shall perish, and rebellion is as the sin of witch-craft, and disobedience as the crime of idolatry. The knight goeth and returneth at the behest of him who is the commander; he clotheth himself with whatsoever hath been assigned to him, and doth not take in advance any kind of clothing or food. And in food and clothing everything super-fluous is avoided, and necessity alone is consulted.

The life of the knights is passed in pleasant association and sober converse with one another, without wives and without children. And lest there should be any lack of evangelic perfection, they without any attention to private rights dwell in one style in one house, anxious to keep the unity of the Spirit in the bond of peace. Thou wouldest say that the whole multitude are of one heart and of one mind, so that each endeavoureth not at all to follow his own will, but rather to be obedient to the will of his commander. At no time do they sit idle, or wander about out of curiosity, but always when they are not moving onwards (which however rarely happeneth) lest they should eat unearned bread, they repair the defects of their weapons or of their clothing, or refashion such things as are worn out, or bring into order what hath got into confusion, and attend in fine to whatsoever the wish of the commander or common necessity may point out as needing to be put right. Amongst them no person is at all favoured. The better one is chosen, not the one more nobly born. They in honour prefer one another : they bear one another's burdens, that they may thus fulfil the law of Christ.

An insolent word, a useless act, a burst of unrestrained laughter, a murmur even slight, or even a whisper to no purpose, when noticed, is not left uncorrected. Draughts and dice they detest; hunting they abhor. They delight not in bird-snaring, though the sport is one generally liked. Comic actors, and sorcerers, and reciters of tales, they have no welcome for. Songs of buffoonery and stage-plays they reject and abominate as vanities and insanities altogether false. They cut their hair short, knowing from the Apostle that it is a shame to a man to cultivate long hair.

Moreover when war threateneth they fortify themselves inwardly with faith, outwardly with steel, not with gold ; to the intent that armed and not adorned they may strike fear into the enemy and not provoke avarice. They desire to have horses strong and swift, but not attractive and adorned with trappings ; thinking forsooth of fighting and not of display, of victory but not of glory, and striving to arouse fear rather than admiration. Then, not with turbulence or impetuosity, but ordering themselves advisedly, with every care and forethought, they place themselves in battle array. But when the actual conflict hath commenced, they at last put aside their former deliberateness, as if they should say : " Do not I hate them, O Lord, who hate Thee, and am not I at war with those who are hostile to Thee?" They rush upon their foes, in no wise fearing, if they themselves are very few in number, either wild barbarians or a numerous multitude. They know at least not to count too much on their own

strength, but to hope for victory from the strength
of the Lord of Sabaoth, with whom, according to
the words of Machabæus, they know it is very
easy for many to be shut up in the hands of
a few; knowing too that it is not different in the
sight of the God of heaven to deliver with many
or with a few, since not in the multitude of an
army is the victory of battle, but in the strength
that cometh from heaven. What also they have
frequently experienced, is this, that one thousand
have pursued after ten thousand, and that two
thousand have put ten thousand altogether to
flight. So that at last they are seen in a certain
marvellous and singular way to be both gentler
than lambs and fiercer than lions; and I forsooth
should almost hesitate whether I ought to call
them monks or knights, unless I might perchance
more consistently call them both, from whom it is
known that there is wanting neither the gentleness of the monk nor the bravery of the knight.
Concerning which thing what can be said, except
that this hath God done and it is marvellous in
our eyes? Such hath God chosen to Himself,
and gathered from the ends of the earth as servants from amongst the bravest of Israel, so that
they may faithfully guard the resting-place of the
true Solomon—forsooth the Holy Sepulchre—all
with swords in their hands, all prepared for battle.

XXI. SAINT BERNARD AND
THREE SAINTLY MAIDENS.

To the Maiden Sophia.

I rejoice with thee, my daughter, in the glory
of thy virtue, by which thou hast spurned the
misleading glory of the world.   That indeed is to
be deservedly refused.   But since many in other
ways wise, in their esteem of the glory of the
world become unwise, thou mayest rightly be
praised because thou art not misled.   Thou art
blessed amongst those that are noble, since, while
others contend for earthly glory, thou by despising
this glory, art more gloriously exalted, and more
exaltedly made glorious.   Of a surety thou art
the more distinguished and illustrious because
thou hast made thyself one of those who are of
small repute, rather than because thou hast
sprung from the midst of the earth's great ones.
For the one is thine own doing by the gift of God :
the other is due to thy forefathers.   Moreover
that which is thine own is so much the more
precious as it is the more rare.

Let others then who have not the hope which is thine, vie with each other for the worthless and diminutive little glory of fleeting and deceitful things. But do thou rest upon the hope that doth not lead to confusion.

Be not desirous of rivalling those perverse ones who borrow a beauty not their own when they have lost their own. Silk and purple and dyed colours have a beauty of their own, but they do not impart it to one arrayed with them. Whatever such thou dost put on the body setteth forth its own beauty, but doth not confer it to the body. It taketh away with it all its beauty when itself is removed. Necessarily a beauty which is put on with a vesture, is without doubt the beauty of the vesture, not of the one who is clothed with it.

Be not as those who indeed show how deprived they are of inborn, inward beauty, when at great study and cost they make a to do to apply to themselves externally the diverse and varied bewitchments of the fashion of the world which passeth away, so that they may appear attractive in the eyes of foolish ones. Count it a thing unworthy of thee to borrow beauty from the furs of ermines and from the toils of worms. Let thine own comeliness be sufficient for thee. For that is the real and genuine beauty of anything which it hath in itself, without any material

lending help. With what a comely bloom doth
the inborn gem of modesty suffuse a maiden's
cheeks! What ear-rings of queens are to be compared to this? Nor doth culture bestow a sign
of lesser comeliness. How culture and discipline
impart calmness to the whole bodily attitude of
a maiden, and not less to the disposition of her
mind! This culture, this discipline, straighteneth
the neck, keepeth undisturbed the brows, com-
poseth the countenance, controlleth the eyes,
withholdeth laughter, restraineth the tongue,
bridleth the appetite, calmeth wrath, giveth grace
to the movements. With such pearls of modesty
it becometh thy robe to be adorned.

Maidenhood encircled with such varied refine-
ments, what is there to whose glory it is not
deservedly to be preferred? To the glory of
angels? An angel hath virginity, but not a
material body. In this respect an angel hath
indeed more of happiness than of virtue. That
adornment then is best and most to be desired,
which even by angels can be longed for.

But consider also another matter of like
import. Thou seest forsooth some who are not
so much adorned as burdened with gold, silver,
and precious stones, and indeed with everything
that appertaineth to queenly splendour. Thou
seest them trailing long robes behind them, of

most costly materials, and stirring up dense clouds of dust in the air. Let not these things attract thee. Such things they will lay aside in death ; but thy sanctity will not leave thee. The things which they carry about are not their own. The world, whose the things are, will keep them, while they themselves will depart hence deprived of all. The world, with the same things of vanity, will beguile others, in like manner vain. But not such is thine own adornment. That will remain with thee, because it is thine. That doth not yield to violence. That cannot be assailed by craft. That is not consumed by moth, or corrupted by age, or worn away by use. In death it liveth on. It is the soul's, not the body's, and dieth not with the body. Moreover even they who kill the body, have nothing that they can do to the soul.

*   *   *

To another Saintly Maiden.

Great is the joy to me in that I hear that thou art willing to reach forward to the true and perfect joy which is not of earth but of heaven ; that is, not of this vale of weeping, but of that city of God which the streams from the river thereof make glad. For compared with that joy, every gladness from elsewhere is sorrow, every pleasure is pain, all sweetness is bitterness, all beauty is worthless, every other thing whatsoever able to delight is a cause of trouble. Doth not the Holy Spirit speak of this in thine heart? Hath not the truth of this persuaded thee, coming from Him before it was uttered by me? For how couldest thou, a woman, young and fair, and full of animation, have thus overcome thy sex and thy years so tender? How couldest thou have thus despised thine acceptable beauty and thy birth so high,— how, unless all things which are subject to the bodily senses were worthless in comparison with those which inwardly strengthen thee, so that thou mayest overcome aught else, and delight thee so that thou preferrest them to others?

Poor and transitory and earthly are the things that thou despisest; but the things that thou desirest are grand, eternal, heavenly. Thou hast left the darkness, and drawn nigh to the light. Thou hast passed from death unto life. For thou wast till now living out thine own will, not the will of God; under thine own law, not under God's; while living thou wast dead—living to the world, but dead to God; or rather, that I may speak with more truth, living neither to the world nor to God. Wishing indeed under the habit and name of religion to spend thy days like one in the world, thou alone hadst driven God from thee by thine own willingness. But not being able

to accomplish what thou foolishly wished, it was
not thou that rejected the world, but the world
that rejected thee. Therefore, rejecting God, and
rejected by the world, thou hadst fallen between
two stools. And so thou wast not living unto
God, because thou wouldest not ; and not to the
world, because thou couldest not ; desiring indeed
the one, refused a welcome by the other ; but yet
dead to both.

Yet now henceforth neither will thy purity of
body be weakened by faultiness in mind ; nor
will thy title of virgin be obscured by faultiness
of manners. From this time neither will the
designation be a false one, nor the veil thou
wearest be devoid of meaning. For why before
this hast thou been called nun and holy sister,
when nevertheless, under thy very name of sanctity,
thy way of life hath not been holy? Why did
the veil on thy head give the lie to the reverence
which should have been thy due, and why
beneath thy veil did thine eye look forth with
eager passion, with unbecoming glances? Thine
head thou didst veil, but thou didst bear it elate.
From beneath the outward sign of modesty thy
tones were otherwise than modest. Thine unrestrained laughter, thy flaunting bearing, thy
clothing with its adornments, would have been
more in harmony with a rich head-dress than

with a veil. But lo ! now at the leading of Christ
the old things have passed away, and all things
begin to be made new ; while thou transformest
care for the exterior into care for the soul within,
and desirest rather to live beautifully than to
dress beautifully. Thou art doing what thou
oughtest to do ; yea, what thou oughtest to have
done in the past ; for thou hadst then vowed to
do it. But the Holy Spirit, which as it breatheth
where it willeth also breatheth when it willeth,
had not yet breathed on thee. And therefore
perchance for what hitherto thou hast done, thou
hast been pardoned. May the same Spirit quench
in thee all carnal desires, so that the holy affections so late conceived, may not by such desires
be stifled !

*   *   *

To a Saintly Maiden of the Convent of
St Mary of Troyes.

It is told to me that thou wishest to leave thy
convent in thy desires for a severer life. Thou
mayest in this have a zeal towards God, so that
thine intention may be pardonable. But how such
a wish as thine can be fulfilled prudently, I do
not at all see. "Why so?" thou dost ask. "Is
it not a wise thing that I should flee from wealth
and from the crowd of a city, and from comforts

63

and delights? Will not my purity be safer in the desert, where dwelling in peace with only a few, or perhaps alone, I may please Him alone to whom I have offered myself?" Not at all. For to one wishing to live reproachfully, the desert hath abundant opportunities, the wood its shade, the solitude its silence. The ill that no one seeth, no one contendeth against. Where no fault-finder is feared, the tempter draweth nigh more securely, wrong-doing is more easily entered upon. But in a convent, if thou doest aught that is good, no one hindereth thee; but if thou wishest to do evil, it is not permitted. Thy wish to do wrong is soon known to many, is rebuked, is corrected. So, on the contrary, when they see good done, they all unitedly admire, reverence. Thou seest, therefore, my daughter, that in a convent both a larger renown followeth thy deeds of merit, and correction followeth more speedily thy faults; since there are there both those to whom thou affordest an example by good deeds, and those whom thou offendest by evil deeds.

I will however take from thee every excuse for thine error, by the Gospel narrative of the two kinds of virgins. Either thou art one of the foolish virgins, or one of the wise. If one of the foolish, thy convent is necessary for thee; if one of the wise, thou art necessary to the convent. For if thou art wise and approved of, the change which hath been newly adopted, and now everywhere praised, will be reported badly of, and will lose support, by thy withdrawal. It will be said, forsooth, that since thou art good, thou wouldest not withdraw from where the good rule was well heeded. If thou hast been known to be foolish, and if thou dost quit the convent, we shall say that because it is not permitted to thee to live wrongly with those who are good, and thy perverseness not enduring the companionship of the good, thou seekest to live where thou mayest live as it pleaseth thee. We shall speak so, justly. For before the reform of the Order, thou didst never, they say, talk thus ; but when duties grew severer, thou suddenly becomest holier, dost begin to think with rapid fervour of the desert. I note in this, my daughter,—I note, would that thou too didst note with me,—the poison of the serpent, the cunning of the crafty one, the astuteness of his changing skin. In the wood dwelleth the wolf. If thou, a little sheep, penetratest the shades of the wood alone, it will seem as thou didst wish to be a prey of the wolf. But hearken to me, my daughter, hearken to my faithful counsel, whether sinner, whether saint, separate not thyself from the flock, lest when the wolf seizeth upon thee there be no one to snatch thee from his grip.

SAINT BERNARD

Art thou a saint? Strive by thine example to
win companions in sanctity. Art thou a sinner?
Do not willingly add sins to sins, but abide in
penitence where thou art, lest by departing with
peril to thyself, as I have shown, thou both leavest
behind a scandal for thy sisters, and provokest
against thyself the tongues of many scornful ones.

XXII. SAINT BERNARD
AND THE DUKE AND DUCHESS
OF LORRAINE.

*To the Duke and Duchess of Lorraine, Bernard,
Abbot of Clairvaux, sendeth greeting, and
desireth that they so delight in one another's
loving and pure affection that the love of
Christ may be the surpassing love of both.*

From the time when we began to send into
your country for the provision of our needs, we
have found in the eyes of your Highnesses much
kindliness and liberality. The blessings of your
generosity ye have freely manifested, when there
was need, upon our brethren. On their crossing
your borders, ye have freely remitted to bearers
of our merchandise, customs, duties, and whatsoever else lawfully cometh to you. For all these
things, without doubt your reward will be great in
heaven.

But why do ye permit your officers to demand
back what ye bestow? Would it not be worthy
and honourable of you, if whatsoever it hath

pleased you to grant for the salvation of your souls, no one should dare to ask for again? If therefore your beneficence is not repented of, and if the gift which with your good pleasure we have often received from you, ye are both pleased that we shall still retain, will ye order your intention to be carried out firmly and unalterably, that henceforth our brethren may not have to fear to be disturbed in this matter by any one of your officers. Otherwise we do not refuse to follow the example of our Lord, who did not disdain to pay tribute money. This we will do willingly, especially because we ought, according to the Apostle, not so much to desire a gift, as that your gain may abound.

XXIII. SAINT BERNARD AND
POPE INNOCENT II.

[1133 ...... 42.]

May the health of the head spread itself
amongst the members. May the oil which de-
scendeth to the beard from the head flow down
even to the lowest skirts of the clothing. If the
sheep are scattered when the shepherd is smitten,
may they, when he is strong and recovered,
return, free from all alarm, to their pasture.
This is what I desire to say. Heraldings not
a few of your frequent glorious successes make
glad the city of God. It is therefore right that
your prosperity should be the Church's fortifying,
and that when God exalteth the chosen of His
people, she also may feel herself to be exalted
and know herself to be stronger by an increase of
strength. For if she have suffered with him she
ought also to reign with him. If amidst fear
and misfortune the vigour of justice hath not
languished, if its zeal hath not cooled, are we to
yield now when we are approaching the goal?

Shall the valour which was conspicuous amid weakness give way in the midst of exaltation?

* * *

Most sweet Father, while we sigh for your presence, we talk gently with each other of the remembrance of your abundant tenderness ; because we crave the one and are consoled by the other. This remembrance is ever in our minds ; it is frequently in our mouths, it is salt to every speech, it sootheth the ear, it reneweth and warmeth our hearts ; it is constantly in the assemblings of the saints, it is the theme of their conversations, it giveth fulness to their petitions, it imparteth eagerness to their prayers. I pray now earnestly for you and yours that the Eternal, with whom and for whom you toil temporarily may keep you worthy of everlasting remembrance. Amen.

XXIV. SAINT BERNARD AND MASTER HENRY MURDACH.

For his beloved Henry Murdach, Bernard, called Abbot of Clairvaux, wisheth health.

What marvel is there, if thou dost waver between prosperity and adversity, who hast not yet placed thy feet upon the rock? But if thou art stedfastly resolved to keep the judgments of the Lord's righteousness, what of these things shall be able to separate thee from the love of Christ? O if thou didst but know and I could declare! "Eye hath not seen, apart from Thee, O God, what Thou hast prepared for them that love Thee."

O if I could be rewarded by having thee ever as my companion in this school of piety under the Master Jesus! O if it were permitted to me to pour into the vessel of thine heart already purified the unction which teacheth of all things! Would that if on me any drop of His gracious rain which He hath stored up for His inheritance, God would at any time of His sweetness deign to distil for me in my lowliness. Would that I could then soon pour it forth upon thee, and in turn receive again from thee that which thou wouldest have had experience of. Believe me who hath tried. Thou wilt find something more in woods than in books. Trees and rocks will teach thee what thou canst not hear from a master. Thinkest thou not that thou canst draw with thy lips honey from the rock and oil from the hardest stone? Do not the mountains distil sweetness, the hills flow with milk and honey, and the valleys abound with corn? With so many things rushing upon me to say to thee, I scarcely can restrain myself. But since thou seekest not a lecture but a prayer, may the Lord open thy heart towards His law and towards His precepts. Farewell.

XXV. SAINT BERNARD AND PRIOR THOMAS OF BEVERLEY.

Bernard to his beloved son Thomas, who is indeed as it were his son.

Words—what is their usefulness? The tongue alone doth not suffice for a fervent spirit and a vehement desire to express themselves. Thine affection and thy visible presence can speak to me. Thou wilt know me better when thou art present with me, and we shall the better know one another. In mutual ties have we been long held as debtors to each other. I to thee must render faithful care, thou to me humble obedience. Let duty done, not the pen, prove both me and thee.

Thy presence I desire. Thy wished-for presence I seek. Thy promised presence I demand. Why such urgency? Not at all do I seek merely thy bodily presence. Either to be profited by thee, or to be useful to thee—such I aim at. Nobleness of blood, loftiness of stature, comeliness of form, the attractiveness of youth, land,

73

palaces, an array of furniture, dignified decorations; add also the wisdom of this world,—of the world are all these, and the world loveth what is its own. But for how long?

The days of man are short. The world indeed passeth away, with its lusts; but it sendeth thee away before itself passeth. How can a love soon to be ended be an endless delight to thee? But thee I love, not thy wealth. Let this go whence it came. Be mindful of thy promise, and no longer deny me the fulness of thy presence, with me who loveth thee sincerely and wilt love thee for ever. In truth loving thee with a pure love in this life, in death also we shall not be divided.

XXVI. ST BERNARD AND
THOMAS OF ST OMER.

To his dearly-beloved son Thomas, Brother Bernard, called Abbot of Clairvaux, sendeth desires that he may walk in the spirit of fear.

Thou doest well by acknowledging the debt of thy promise, and by not denying that thou art guilty in delaying its fulfilment. But I wish thee to think not only of what thou promised, but also of Him to whom thou didst make the promise. For I usurp to myself nothing of that which was made in my presence, and do thou consider that thy promise was not made to me, though made in my presence. Thou hast transgressed. What is that to me? To thy Lord thou standest or fallest.

Alas! alas! thou seemest to me to walk in the same spirit, just as also thou art known by the same name, with that other Thomas, once forsooth Prior of Beverley, who when he had devoted himself with entire zeal to our Order and our monastery, began to act disappointingly and so

75

little by little to wane into coldness, until he became a worldling and insincere, and a twofold child of the region of loss, and was snatched away before his time by a sudden and shocking death. Let the merciful and compassionate Lord, if it be possible, turn him away from that realm of loss.

If thou art wise, his lack of wisdom will be for thee a warning from which thou wilt profit

XXVII. SAINT BERNARD AND BISHOP ARDUTIUS OF GENEVA.

[1135 ...... 44.]

Charity bestoweth on me boldness to speak to thee with faithfulness. The cathedral throne which hath lately fallen to thy lot demandeth a man of many parts. None of these, or not sufficient of them, I grieve dwelt aforehand in thee. Indeed thy doings and thy past pursuits have seemed in no wise to lead on fittingly towards episcopal duties. What then? Cannot God of this stone raise up a son of Abraham? Is not God able to cause that the good deeds which ought to have gone before shall certainly follow after? This we certainly and freely accept, if perchance it so happeneth. For, though I know not how, such a sudden change wrought by the right hand of the Most High will be more pleasing than if the excellences of thy former life recommended thee. Then may I say, forsooth, "This is the Lord's doing, and it is marvellous in our eyes." Thus Paul from a persecutor was made a teacher of the Gentiles. Thus Matthew was called from the tax office, thus Ambrose was hurried away from his palace, the one to an apostleship, the other to the toils of a bishop. Thus have I known many others who have been singled out and promoted from secular life and

77

its occupations. Hath it not indeed been often
thus, that where there hath been superabund-
ance of failure there it hath been seen that grace
hath also pre-eminently abounded?

Thus, then, friend most dear, animated by
these and such-like examples, gird up thy loins
like a man. Choose henceforth the pathways of
goodness, and be zealous in deeds of excellence;
so that thy newest deeds may lull thy former ones
to sleep, and the righteousness of thine eventide
may banish the shortcomings of thy youth. Take
care to imitate Paul in rendering honour to thy
ministry. Thou wilt render honour to it by
seriousness of manners, by maturity of counsel,
by honourableness of deed. These are the things
which chiefly ennoble and adorn the office of a
bishop. Do all things with the advice, not indeed of
all, or of any soever, but of good men only. Have
thou good men for thy counsellors, for thy fol-
lowers, for thy household, who may be both the
guardians and the witnesses of thy life and of
thine honour. For in this thou wilt prove thyself
to be good, if thou shalt have the testimony of
the good. Let there be commended to thy piety
our poor brethren, who are around thee, dwellers
in the Alps at Bonnemont and at Hautecombe.
By thy kindness to these I shall learn how great
is thy regard for myself.

XXVIII. SAINT BERNARD AND THE MONKS OF CLAIRVAUX.

[1135 ...... 44.]

*To his dearest brethren, the Monks of Clairvaux,
the Converts, and the Novices, Brother Bernard sendeth greeting; and his desire that
they may rejoice in the Lord always.*

Consider what I am suffering from you. If
my absence is grievous to you, let no one doubt
that it is more grievous to myself. For that ye
should be without me only, and that I should be
bereft of the society of you all, are not equal
losses, are not the same burdens. Of a necessity
I am touched with the feeling of as many cares
as ye are in number, and I grieve over the
absence of each one of you from myself, and fear
the dangers that may befall each. This twofold
distress will not quit me until I am restored to
my dear children. Thus also indeed I doubt not
that ye feel for me. But I am one only. On
you there presseth one cause of sadness, on myself a multiplicity, by reason, forsooth, of you
all. And not only is it a torment that I am

79

compelled to live for a time without you, away
from whom even to reign I should deem to be
miserable servitude; but also that I am compelled to busy myself with those things which
altogether disturb the serenity of friendship, and
are perchance least in accord with my cherished
aim.

Knowing these things it behoveth you not to
be vexed with me, but to feel compassion for me,
because of my long absence, which is not of mine
own will, but is of ecclesiastical necessity. But I
hope that it will not be long. Do ye pray that it
may not be unfruitful. Let losses which meanwhile may happen to you be counted as gains,
since they will be in God's cause. He, since He
is merciful and able to do all things, will easily
replace losses, replacing not only with exactness
but with an over-abundance of gifts. Let us,
therefore, having God with us, be of good heart.
In Him also I am present with you, though we
may seem to be severed by ever so long earthly
distances. Whosoever among you manifesteth a
spirit of dutifulness, humility, and reverence, and
who is zealous in his reading, watchful in his
prayers, and devoted in brotherly love, let him
not think that from him I am absent. For am
I not present in spirit to him with whom I am of
one heart and of one mind? But if amongst you

there dwell any whisperer (may such be far from you!) or any that is double-tongued, or a murmurer, or defiant, or impatient of discipline, or unquiet and disposed to wander, and who in idleness blusheth not to eat bread; from him, even if I should be present with him in body, my soul would be far off, inasmuch as he would have caused himself to be far off from God, by distance of disposition and not of space.

In the meanwhile, brothers, until I come, serve the Lord in fear, that when set free from the hand of your enemies, ye may serve Him without fear. Serve Him in hope, since He is faithful in His promises. Serve Him by worthy deeds, since He aboundeth in rewards.

Although I be silent about other things, as to this of a certainty I must not be. He claimeth our service. He asketh for our life for Himself, since for it He offered His own. Let no one therefore live for himself, but for Him who hath died for him. For whom surely may I more justly live than for Him, who if He had not died, I should not have life? For whom may I live looking for greater reward, than for Him who promiseth eternal life? I serve Him willingly because love giveth liberty. Therefore, my children, serve Him in that love which casteth out fear, which is conscious of no toils, which seeketh not reward, which requireth not any incentive, and yet impelleth more than all. No terror maketh so eager an appeal, no rewards so invite, no justice demandeth so much. May that love unite you to me inseparably, may it continually make you conscious that I am with you, especially in the hours in which ye are at prayer, dearest and much longed for brethren.

*   *   *

My soul is sad until I return, and it will not be consoled till then. For what is my consolation in the time of evil, and in the place of my pilgrimage? Are not ye so, in the Lord? Not in the least, wheresoever I go, doth the sweet remembrance of you leave me; but the sweeter the remembrance the more painful the absence. Alas! for me, that my sojourning here is not only prolonged but also made more burdensome.

One solace hath aforetime been given to me from above, that I should see the holy temple of God, which ye are. What shall I say? How often hath that solace been taken from me! Lo! this is the third time, unless I am in error, that my children have been torn from me. My little ones have been weaned before the time; those whom I have begotten through the Gospel, it is not permitted to me to bring up. Mine own I am compelled to abandon, and to take upon me the care of others; and I doubt which I bear the more bitterly, to be withdrawn from mine own, or to be involved with the others.

Is thus, good Jesus, my whole life to be wasted with grief and my years with mourning? It is good for me, O Lord, rather to die than to live, and not however except amongst my brethren, amongst those who are of one house with me, amongst my dearest friends. That indeed is clearly sweeter, with more of human sweetness, with more of loving protection. Yea, indeed, it would be an act of Thy love to grant to me that I might thus be refreshed before I go away, and be here no more. If it please my Lord, that the eyes of such a father as I am, who am not worthy to be called a father, should be closed by the hands of sons, that they may see his last moments, console his departure, and lift up his spirit by their longings, if thou shouldest deem him worthy, to the fellowship of the blessed, and bury his body with the bodies of the poor and lowly,—this, truly, if I have found favour in Thy sight, I desire with full yearning to obtain by the prayers and merits of these my brethren. Nevertheless not my will but Thine be done! Not for myself wish I to live or to die!

But it is fitting that ye who hear of my sor-

row should not be ignorant of my consolation, if
such there is. First, indeed, in every toil and
calamity which I endure, I think that all is borne
in the cause of Him in whom alone all things
live. Whether I will or not, it is needful for me
to live for Him who hath bought my life with His
own: who also as a merciful and just Judge, is
able, if in anything we suffer for Him, to reward
us. If I have served Him willingly there is glory
for me.

My next solace is that often, not with merits
of mine own, grace from on high hath honoured
me in my labours and that grace in me was not
a mere appearance, as I have in many things
found, and as hath not in some part been hidden
from you. But, also, in these days, how necessary to the Church of God may be or shall be the
presence of my feebleness, I would tell you for
your consolation, if it would not savour of self-
glorying. But now it is better that this ye should
know from others.

Induced by the urgent demand of the Em-
peror, by the Apostolic command, and also by the
prayers of the Church and of the princes, sadly
and unwillingly, feeble and ill, and, that I may
speak the truth, carrying about with me the pallid
image of alarming death, I am borne away to
Apulia. Pray ye for the things which belong to

the peace of the Church, pray ye for the things which are needful for my salvation, that I may see you again and may live with you, and die with you; and so live that ye may obtain. In illness and in time of anxiety, certainly with tears and laments, I have dictated these words— as he can witness who hath taken them down with the pen, our dear Brother Baldwin, whom the Church hath called to another office and to another dignity. Pray also for him as mine only comfort, and in whom my spirit findeth much rest. Pray for our Lord the Pope, who cherisheth me equally with all of you with paternal affection. Pray also for the Lord Chancellor, who to me is as a mother, and for those who are with him, my Lord Luke, and my Lord Chrysogonus, and Master Ivo, who act towards me as mine own brothers. Brother Bruno and Brother Gerard who are with me, salute you, and beseech you to pray for them.

XXIX. SAINT BERNARD PREACHING TO HIS MONKS.

From a Sermon.

Since I sometimes speak to you oftener than what hath been the custom of our Order, I do not so from presumption, but at the wish of my venerable brothers and fellow Abbots, who enjoin me to do even that which they are unwilling generally to permit to themselves. They know in truth that another method and a special necessity are enforced upon me. For I should not now be speaking to you, if I were able to be working with you. That would perchance be of more benefit to you, and also more in accord with my conscience. But since that is denied to me through my sins, and through the manifold infirmities of the burdened body (as ye yourselves know), and also by the lack of time, may I, speaking and not doing, deserve to be found, certainly least in the kingdom of God. Amen.

*   *   *

Will, Reason, Memory.

Eye hath not seen, O God, apart from Thee, the things which Thou hast prepared for them that love Thee. Tell us then Thou who preparest, what Thou preparest. We believe, we are assured, the very things that Thou dost promise. "We shall be filled with the good things of Thine house." But with which good things? With what kind of good things? Is it perchance with corn, wine, and oil, with gold and silver, and precious stones? But these things we have known and seen. We both see them, and are wearied of them. We seek that which eye hath not seen, which ear hath not heard, and which hath not ascended into the heart of man. This pleaseth, this is sweet, this delighteth us to enquire into, whatsoever it may be. All shall be taught of God, and He will be all in all. As I give heed to this, the fulness which we expect from God will not be except of God.

But who may grasp how great a fulness of delight is comprehended in this brief word, "God will be all in all"? That I may be silent as to the body, I discern in the soul three things—

87

reason, will, memory; and these three are the
soul itself. How much of these to one in the
present life is wanting, in integrity and perfection, every one feeleth who walketh in the
Spirit. Why is this, unless it is because God is
not yet all in all? Hence it is that reason also
very often faileth in judgment, and will is tossed
about with fourfold perturbation, and memory
confoundeth us by manifold forgetfulness. To
this threefold failing a noble creature is subject,
but not willingly, and withal in hope. For
He who filleth with good things the desire
of the soul, will Himself be to reason the fulness of light, will Himself be to the will the
abundance of peace, will Himself be to memory
eternal unfaltering continuance. O truth! O
charity! O eternity! O blessed and blessing
trinity! To thee my miserable trinity—the trinity
of my reason, will, and memory—miserably be-
waileth, since from thee it is unhappily exiled.
Separating itself from thee, in what great errors,
sorrows and fears, it is involved! What sort of a
trinity have we in exchange for thee? My heart
is disturbed, and hence my sorrow; my strength
hath forsaken me, and hence my fear; the light
of mine eyes is not with me, and hence my error.
Lo! what a transformed trinity, O trinity of my
soul, dost thou show to me in mine exile!

But "Why art thou cast down, O my soul, and why art thou disquieted within me? Hope thou in God, for I will yet put my trust in Him." This will I do when error shall have fled from my reason, sorrow from my will, and every fear from my memory, and there shall have succeeded to them the things that we hope for, wondrous serenity, abundant sweetness, and eternal overflowing steadfastness. The first of these will be accomplished by the God of truth, the second by the God of love, the third by the God of highest power. They will be so accomplished that God will be all in all; the reason receiving light inextinguishable, the will attaining peace unshakeable, the memory being ever refreshed by a fountain that will not fail. See ye, whether ye may rightly assign the first to the Son, the second to the Holy Spirit, the last to the Father; so however that ye take away nothing from any one of them, from the Father, or from the Son, or from the Holy Spirit.

XXX. SAINT BERNARD AND THE CISTERCIAN ABBOTS.

[1137 ...... 46.]

To the Abbots assembled at Citeaux.

In much feebleness of body and anxiety of mind, God knoweth, I have dictated these words for you,—I a man poor, a man born to toil, yet your brother. Would that I might deserve to have now the Holy Spirit, in whom ye have assembled together, as my Intercessor to you in your re-union, that He might impress upon your hearts the calamity that I suffer, that He might present to your brotherly affection my sad and suppliant image, as it now is. I do not pray this, that He will create in you a new mercifulness, since I know how familiar to you all is that virtue: but this I pray, that ye may in your inmost hearts feel with what deep love there is need for me to be pitied. For I am certain that if it were given to you so to feel, tears would without cease break forth from the shrine of your love, that lamentations and sighs would sound towards heaven, and that God would hear, and would show pleasure towards me, and say "I have restored thee to thy brethren: thou shalt not die amongst strangers, but in the midst of thine own."

I am so affected by my so great labours and griefs, that often it is weary to me even to live. But I speak as a man by reason of mine infirmity. I desire to linger until I return to you, that I may not die unless amongst you. For the rest, brethren, make good your ways and your endeavours, deciding upon and clinging to the things that are right, that are honourable, that are wholesome in influence. Before all things be anxious to keep the unity of the Spirit in the bond of peace; and may the God of peace be with you.

XXXI. SAINT BERNARD AND HIS BROTHER GERARD.

[1138 ...... 47.]

Bernard resumed his exposition of " The Song of Songs," but soon broke away from his theme into an impassioned lamentation for his brother Gerard.

How long am I to dissemble? How long shall the flame which I hide within me burn up my sad heart, feed upon mine innermost soul? Though pent up within me, it windeth around in whirls, it rageth very fiercely. What is this canticle to me now that I am in bitter sorrow? The strength of my sorrow taketh away from me all mine intentness, and the indignation of the Lord exhausteth my spirit. Inasmuch as there hath been taken from me him by whom my studies for the Lord's sake were wont to be in some way allowed freedom, my heart also hath at the same time left me. But up till now I have restrained my soul, and have hidden its sorrow, lest affection should seem to overpower faith. While others were weeping, I, as ye could see, with tearless eyes followed in the mournful procession, with tearless eyes stood at the grave, until all the solemnities of the rite were ended. Robed in my priestly vestments,

I, with mine own lips, completed the appointed prayers for him; with mine own hands, as is the custom, I cast earth upon the body of my beloved, soon to become earth itself. They who looked upon me wept, and marvelled that I myself did not weep, since they all pitied, not indeed him, but myself rather who had lost him. For whose heart there, even had it been made of iron, would not have been moved for me, seeing me deprived of Gerard? All had suffered loss, but by the side of my sad trouble their own loss was not thought of. Yet I, with what energy faith could command, combated my feelings, striving not to be moved against my resolve to a vain resistance to the behest of Nature, to the debt due from all, to the lot appertaining to our condition, to the ordering of the Almighty, to the judgment of the Just One, to the stroke of Him whom all must fear, to the will of the Lord. Thus I then and afterwards compelled myself, though very distressed and sad, not to indulge in much weeping. Still I who was able to restrain my tears, could not overcome my sadness; as it is written, "I was distressed, and I spake not." But the grief suppressed rooted itself more deeply inwardly and, as I feel, became the bitterer, the more it was not permitted to utter itself. I confess now I am overcome. What I suffer inwardly must come forth outwardly. Let it come forth then before the eyes of my sons, who knowing my bereavement, will think kindly of my lamenting, will more sweetly console.

Ye know, O my sons, how justifiable is my grief, how agonising is my wound. Assuredly ye discern how faithful was the companion who hath left me in the way in which I was walking, how he was watchful amid cares, how he was diligent in toil, how he was gentle in all his ways. Who thus was more essentially necessary to me? By whom was I so beloved? Brother he was by birth, but more closely a brother by religion. Grieve, I pray you, over my fate, you to whom these things are known. Weak I was in body, and he supported me; faint I was in heart, and he encouraged me; indolent and negligent I was, and he roused me to action; thoughtless and forgetful, and he admonished me. Why art thou torn from me? Why art thou snatched from my hands?—thou ever of one mind with me, thou ever according to mine own heart? We loved one another in life. Why are we separated by death? O bitterest separation! which only death could have wrought! For when didst thou in life ever desert me? Death's work alone it is, this dreadful tearing asunder! For who would not have spared the sweet chain of our love, except death

94

the enemy of every sweetness?—death rightly so
called, which by bearing off one, smiteth with its
fury two! Is not his death also mine? Yea,
more is it mine, as to me the life that remaineth
is more luckless than any death. I live, that
living I may be ever dying; and shall I call this
life? How more kindly thou mightest have deprived me, O cruel Death, of the use of life, than
of its fruit! for life without fruit is harder to be
borne than death. A twofold ill is at last prepared for the unfruitful tree, axe and fire. Envy-
ing my toils, then, thou hast taken from me my
brother and friend, by whose zeal my labours
were fruitful, if indeed they were so. Better
would it have been for me to have had henceforth my life in danger than to have lost thy
presence, O Gerard, thou who wast as to my
labours in the Lord an anxious encourager, a
faithful helper, a careful counsellor. Why, I ask,
have we loved one another, or why have we lost
one another? How hard it is! But mine is the
lot to be pitied, not his! For thou, dear brother,
as thou hast lost dear ones, thou hast assuredly
welcomed dearer ones. But what consolation
remaineth now for me in my unhappiness after
the loss of thee, my dearest solace? Equally
acceptable to both of us was our association
together in this life, by reason of the harmony of

95

our pursuits; but our separation hath wounded me alone. What was delightful was for us both; what is sad and mournful is mine. Over me hath passed God's wrath; on me hath anger pressed heavily. Each other's welcome presence, sweet companionship, soothing converse, were for both of us; but such delights that I have lost thou hast exchanged for others. And in truth great hath been thy compensation by the change.

What great increase of joys and heaping up of blessings are thine, dearest brother, as thou art deprived of me! Thou hast certainly had bestowed on thee in the place of me in my exceeding littleness, the presence of Christ; and thou dost not feel loss from thine absence from me, mingling as thou dost in choirs of angels. It is not therefore for thee to complain of my presence being as it were taken from thee, since the Lord of glory hath granted unto thee abundantly the fulness of His presence and the joy of the presence of His blessed ones. But I, what have I instead of thee? How I desire to know what thou feelest now of me, thy dearest brother, as I stumble amid cares and troubles, deprived of thee, the staff of my feebleness! If indeed it is permitted to thee to think of those dwelling in sadness, now that thou hast entered into the depths of light, and art absorbed in that sea of eternal felicity. For perchance although thou hast known me in the body, thou dost now no longer know me; and since thou hast entered into the realms of the Lord, thou art mindful of His righteousness only, and art forgetful of mine. He who is united with God is one spirit with Him, and is altogether transformed into a certain divine affection, and is not able now to think or know of anything but God, and as he is full of God, that which he thinks and knows is God. But God is Love, and the more anyone is in union with God, the more is he filled with love. Moreover God is incapable of suffering, but is not uncompassionate: to Him alone it appertaineth ever to have mercy and to spare. So also thou must be merciful, as thou dwellest in the All-merciful One, and although thou art not in any sadness, although thou art one who dost not suffer, yet thou dost enter into the sufferings of others. Thine affection henceforth is not diminished, but changed; and since thou hast entered into the life of God, thou hast not departed out of care for us. What is weak thou hast thrown off, but not what is affectionate. Charity indeed never faileth, and thou wilt not be forgetful of me for ever.

I seem to hear my brother saying, "I will not forget thee." Certainly it would not be well that I should be forgotten. Thou knowest how I am bewildered, how I am cast down, how thou hast left me. There is no one to stretch out a helping hand. At every difficulty I look out for Gerard, as I was wont to do, and he is not nigh. Alas! I then in my unhappiness mourn, as one without help. Whom shall I take counsel with in perplexities? In whom shall I have confidence in the midst of opposition? Who will bear my burdens? Who will thrust dangers out of my path? Did not the eyes of Gerard go before on the way I trod, everywhere? Did not my cares fasten upon more consciously, invade more constantly, press upon more severely, thine heart, Gerard, than upon mine own? Didst thou not very often set free my tongue from worldly speech by means of thine own lips, so peaceful and winning, and thus give me up to my beloved silence?

The Lord had given to him a scholarly and judicious tongue, so that he knew when and how he ought to speak. Thus at last by the prudence of his replies, and by the grace given to him from above, he so won the favour both of those of the house and of strangers, that no one whom by chance Gerard had first met with, had scarcely need to enquire of me. He would indeed accost those who came, intercepting them lest they should suddenly disturb my quietness. If he was unable to satisfy any himself, such he led to me; the others he sent away. O toilsome one! O faithful friend! He would gratify one who came in friendliness, and was also not wanting in the duties of charity. Who went from him with empty hands? If the one who came to him were rich, he would carry away advice; if poor, that which would be assistance.

And he who would plunge into the midst of cares, so that I might be free from care, was not wont to seek the things which were his own. For he used to hope, as he was most humble, that there would be more fruitful results from my quiet hours, than if he himself were free from cares. Sometimes however he would ask to be set free, and would pass on his task to another, as to one who would the better devote himself to it. But where was that one to be found? Nor was he detained in his duty by any petulant feeling, as often happeneth, but by the insight alone of charity. He used to toil, indeed more than all others, and would receive less than all, so that often whilst he ministered things necessary to others, he would himself be wanting in many things, such as food and clothing. At last, when he felt himself drawing nigh to his departure, he prayed thus: "God, Thou knowest that as

far as in me was, I have ever craved for quiet,
to give myself to contemplation, to be free for
communing with Thee. But reverence for Thee,
the wishes of the brethren, and love of obedience,
and above all affection for him who is alike my
Abbot and my brother, have kept me in the
embrace of duty."

So it is. Thanks to thee, my brother, for
every fruitful result, if such there is, of my studies
in the Lord. To thee I owe it if I have advanced, if I have been useful to others. Thou
didst entangle thyself in duties, and I by thy
kindness to me used to sit undisturbed or certainly was able to devote myself more sacredly to
divine services, or to apply myself more usefully
to the instruction of my soul. For how could I
not be inwardly in peace, when I knew that thou
wast acting apart from me as my right hand,
as the light of mine eyes, as mine heart and as my
tongue? Indeed thy hand was unwearied, thine
eye clear, thine heart encouraging, thy tongue
ever speaking wisdom!

But why have I said that Gerard was active
in outward matters, as if he knew nought of
inward things, and were destitute of spiritual
gifts? The spiritually-minded who knew him
were conscious that his words had in them a
spiritual fragrance. His indoor associates knew

that his converse and his aims did not savour of
the flesh, but glowed with the Spirit. Who more
strict than he in obedience to discipline? Who
more severe than he in control of his body, more
ethereal or more lofty in contemplation, more
refined in utterance when teaching? How often
in conferring with him have I learnt things that
I knew not. I who had come to teach another
had gone from him the more instructed myself.
And it is not wonderful that it should be so with
me, when great and wise minds testify that the
same, in no wise to a less degree, had happened
to themselves when with him. He knew not the
learning contained in books, but he had an
insight into the truths of such, and he had also
an illuminating spirit. And not only of the
greatest things was he master; he was familiar
also with the smallest things. What was there
as to building, as to fields, as to gardens, as to
water supply, and indeed as to all the arts and
labours of country people,—what, I say, was there
as to such matters that escaped the knowledge of
Gerard? Over masons, smiths, workers in the
fields, gardeners, shoemakers, and weavers, he
was easily able to take control. And while in the
judgment of all he was wiser than all, in his own
eyes alone he was not wise.

He was useful to me in all things, and before

all others. He was useful in small things and in great, in private matters and in public concerns, outside the walls and within. Rightly did I altogether trust to him, who was all to me. He left to me only the honour and the name of Superior. As to the work that he himself accomplished, I was called Abbot, but he had chief care over it all. Rightly did I inwardly rest on him by whom I was enabled to delight myself in the Lord, to preach more freely, to pray in closer seclusion.

Through thee it was, my brother, that my mind was kept calm, my rest was acceptable, my utterances more useful, my preaching richer with thought, my reading more frequent, my affections more fervent. Alas! thou hast been taken away, and all these things with thee. With thee have gone all my delights, all my joys. Already cares are rushing in, already troubles that before I knew not of are assailing me, and difficulties on every side are overtaking me in my loneliness. These burdens alone have remained to me through thy departure. Under the weight of them, in my solitariness, I lament. Either I must lay them down, or be oppressed by them, since thou hast removed thy shoulders from beneath them. Who will grant to me speedily after thee to die? For to die instead of thee I was unwilling, lest I should defraud thee of thy glory. But labour

and sorrow have survived thee. As long as I
shall live, I shall live on in bitterness. I shall
live on in grief; and let this be my consolation,
that I shall be grieved and afflicted. I will not
spare myself, and I will assist the Lord's hand;
for the hand of the Lord hath touched me.

Me, I say, the Lord hath touched and smitten,
not him whom He hath called to rest. Me He
slew when He took him away. For shall he be
called slain, whom the Lord hath planted in life?
But what to him was the gate of life, to myself
hath plainly been death, and by that death, I
should call dead, myself, not him who hath slept
in the Lord. Flow, flow, tears long wishing to
flow, since he who would have stayed your flowing hath gone. Let the floods of my misery open
out a channel, and let the fountains of waters
break forth, if perchance they may suffice to
cleanse away the stains of my sins, because of
which I have deserved wrath! When the Lord
shall have had mercy upon me, then perchance I
shall deserve to be consoled, if however I refrain
not from mourning; for they who mourn shall be
comforted. Hence, let everyone lovingly sympa-
thetic condescend to me, and he who is spiritually
minded, let him sustain me in my lamentation,
with a manifestation of tenderness. There are in
me no laments as to worldly things. I grieve as

to things which are especially of God—the faithful help taken from me, the sound counsel. I
mourn for Gerard—Gerard, my brother according
to the flesh, but spiritually closer, and my companion in every aspiration.

Since, therefore, we were of one heart and of
one soul, the sword hath pierced my soul and his
soul as well, and cleaving them asunder, hath
placed one part of one soul in heaven, and hath
left the other amid earthly corruption. I, I am
that unhappy portion left in the mire of earth,
and cut off from the part better than I am; and it
is said to me, "Do not weep." Mine heart is torn
from me, and it is said to me, "Do not suffer."
I do suffer, I suffer indeed unwillingly, since
my fortitude is not the fortitude of stones, and
my flesh is not of bronze. I suffer assuredly and
am in sorrow, and my sorrow is ever in my
sight. Gerard hath gone from me. I suffer, I am
wounded, grievously wounded!

Forgive me, my sons; or rather, if ye are my
sons, weep for your father's sadness. Have pity
on me, have pity on me, ye at least who are
my friends, who surely take note, how severe is
the punishment I have received for my sins from
the hand of the Lord.

Who would say that it is a light thing for me
to live without Gerard, except one who knoweth

104

not how Gerard and I were knit together in affection?

I grieve as to thee, dearest Gerard, not because thou art to be grieved about, but because thou hast been taken from me. And therefore perchance I should grieve rather as to myself, I who drink the cup of bitterness, and drink it alone. Would that I may not have lost thee, but only have sent thee on before! Would that, even if it be only slowly, I may follow thee whithersoever thou shalt have gone! For doubtless thou hast gone to those whom towards the middle of thy last night thou didst invite to praise God when with a look and a voice of exultation, thou didst suddenly—to the astonishment of those who stood by—sing out that Psalm of David:

> Praise ye the Lord from the heavens:
> Praise Him in the heights.

For thee, then, my brother, while it was still midnight, the day began to dawn, and the night was illumined as the day. Assuredly that night was thine illumination in the midst of thy delights. I was summoned to look upon that marvel, to see a man exulting in death, triumphing over death. O death, where is thy victory? O death, where is thy sting? Gerard doth not fear thee,

thou shadowy phantom! Gerard passeth through
thy grasp to his fatherland not only in safety, but
joyfully, singing songs of praise. When then I
had come to him and he had finished, as I
listened to him, singing the last verse of the
Psalm, looking up to heaven, he said, "Father,
into Thy hands I commend my spirit." And
repeating the same words, and crying out more
than once, "Father, Father," he turned to me,
and with countenance full of delight, said, "How
great is the condescension of God, in that He is
the Father of men! How great the glory of men
in being sons of God and heirs of God! For if
they are sons they are also heirs." So sang he
whom we mourn; and I confess he changed my
grief almost into joy. Whilst intently noting
his blessedness, I almost forgot mine own unhappiness.

But my grief so piercing recalleth me to
myself, and from that calm vision, as weighty
anxiety arouseth from a light sleep. Let me
grieve, then, but for myself, since reason now
forbiddeth my grieving for him! For I think he
would say to us now, "Weep not for me, but weep
for yourselves."

Though my words are full of grief, they are
not words of murmuring. Have I not fully acknowledged the Lord's justice in that He in the

compass of one sentence hath both punished one deserving of punishment and crowned one meriting reward? And still I say, "The compassionate and righteous Lord hath done well, both with myself and with him. Just art Thou, O Lord, and righteous are Thy judgments. Gerard Thou hast given, Gerard Thou hast taken away; and if we mourn that he hath been taken away, we are not forgetful that he was given and we give thanks that we have been counted worthy of having him with us."

I remember, Lord, my covenant with Thee, and Thy tender mercy. When we were, by reason of Church concerns, at Viterbo last year, Gerard became ill, and in his increasing weakness, his being called hence seemed quite near. I was very sad at the thought of losing the companion of my pilgrimage, of being bereft of him in a strange land, and of not being able to restore him to those who had entrusted him to me—for he was loved by all; he was so lovable. I betook myself to prayer with tears and sobs. "Wait, O Lord," I said, "until my return. Take him, if Thou wilt, when he is restored to his friends, and I will not murmur." Thou didst hear me, O Lord; he recovered. The work which Thou hadst enjoined upon us we accomplished. We returned with joy, bringing

with us the sheaves of peace. Yet afterwards I
became almost forgetful of my covenant with
Thee; but Thou wast not. I am ashamed of
these sobbings, which pronounce me unfaithful.
But what more can I say? Thou hast demanded
him whom Thou hadst committed unto us. Thou
hast received Thine own. Tears stop my words.
Do Thou, O Lord, restrain my tears, and bring
them to an end.

XXXII. SAINT BERNARD AND HIS BRETHREN AT FOUNTAINS.

[1138 ...... 47.]

*To Alexander, Prior of Fountains Abbey, and
to the Brethren of the same place.*

*To the most beloved Brethren in Christ, Alex-
ander the Prior, and all in the Convent of
Fountains, Brother Bernard, called Abbot of
Clairvaux,—health, and prayers such as he
can offer.*

Your venerable Father in a blessed ending
hath finished his course, and hath fallen asleep
in the Lord. But I although always anxious for
you with paternal love as for children of mine own,
do now feel greater solicitude for you by so much
as a greater necessity lieth upon you. Wherefore
I should have also sent to you long ago if I had
not been lingering until more opportunely and
more usefully I might be able to do so, when the
venerable Abbot Henry through being occupied
with sundry matters had not been able to proceed
to you earlier. Him especially I had from the

first intended to destine for this mission, inasmuch as he seemed to me for it better fitted and more likely to be useful than anyone else. Him, therefore, dearest brethren, receive with the honour and love of which he is worthy; and so listen to him in all things, as you would to myself. Yea, rather, so much more do so, as he cometh before me both in prudence and in deserts. And indeed I have entrusted to him altogether the duty both as to carrying on the election, and as to all things whatsoever,—whether in your own monastery, or in others which have sprung from it—that may have to be set in order or to be amended. I have sent also with him Brother William, who is my very dear son.

And now I beseech you, as well-beloved sons, that in the election of your Abbot, ye be all possessed with the same wisdom, and that there be no differences among you, but that ye may with one mind and one mouth glorify God. For He is not a God of dissension, but of peace; whence also His abode hath been established in peace. Let it be far from those who abide in the school of Christ, under the guidance of the Holy Spirit, that the enemy should rejoice over them, and glory in their dissensions, since thus their own souls would be placed in danger, and the whole effort of penitence would be in vain and perish ; and they would cause the good fame of our Order to be smirched, and the name of Christ would be blasphemed through those by whom it should chiefly be glorified. But rather—as I well trust ye will do—choose, I beseech you, as it becometh saints,—choose for yourselves, as it behoveth the servants of Christ, with one mind, a fit Shepherd of your Souls, having associated with you the venerable Abbots of Rievaulx and Valle-Clara, whose counsel I wish you to acquiesce in in all things, as in mine own.

XXXIII. SAINT BERNARD AND ABBOT HENRY MURDACH.

[1138 ...... 47.]

To Henry of Murdach, first Abbot of Valle-Clara,
afterwards of Fountains, and at length
Archbishop of York.

To his dearest brother and fellow Abbot, Henry,
Brother Bernard, called Abbot of Clairvaux,
sendeth greeting and assurance of prayers.

I counsel thee, brother Henry, that if on thee
shall fall the choice of our brethren at Fountains,
with the approval of the venerable Abbot of
Rievaulx, not to refuse, but to obey in charity.
This indeed I advise unwillingly, knowing that
by thine absence I shall be deprived of a great
solace. But I fear to oppose their united choice,
believing that word to come forth from God, in
which the decisions of so many religious are in
harmony, since I read in the Gospel, "Wherever
two or three are gathered together in My name, I
am in the midst of them." Take courage, therefore, dearest brother, and receive their profes-

sions, and for the rest take them under thy care, as the shepherd of their souls. And do not fear, by reason of the house which thou hadst undertaken to rule. For I, God willing, will provide for it a useful guardian, for it is very near to me. But do not hesitate to obey my counsel because of the Bishop. Intrust that matter to me.

XXXIV. SAINT BERNARD AND HUGO, A NOVICE.

[1138 ...... 47.]

To Hugo, a Novice, afterwards Abbot of Bonneval.

To his son, Hugo, very dear in Christ,—a new creature in Christ,—for whom Brother Bernard, called Abbot of Clairvaux, desireth that he may be comforted in the Lord.

Having heard of thy conversion I am filled with joy and delight. Why should not men be glad when also angels rejoice? Already the day is one to be celebrated. Already resound on high the uttered thanks and the voice of praise. A youth, noble, delicate, hath conquered evil, hath despised the world, hath subdued the flesh, hath renounced the love of kindred, hath flown through the nets woven by riches, like one with wings. Whence hast thou this wisdom, my son? For I have not found wisdom so great in the aged of Babylon. For they, according to, or rather in defiance of, the Apostle, haste to be made

114

rich in this world, so that they fall into temptation and into the snare of the evil one. The wisdom of our Hugo is not of earth, but of heaven. I confess to Thee, O Father, that Thou hast hidden these things from the wise, and hast revealed them unto a child.

And do thou, my son, be not ungrateful for the Redeemer's kindness. Let not the strictness of the Order terrify thy tender age. Remember that the rougher the thistle, the smoother is made the cloth by its tousling; the stonier the way of life the tenderer the conscience. The sweetness of Christ shall be thine. He shall be to thee as a mother, and thou shalt be to Him as a son.

Remember in all things to acquiesce in the counsels of thy spiritual fathers, not otherwise than as though such counsels were the precepts of Divine majesty. This do, and thou shalt live. This do, and there shall come upon thee blessings, so that for everything thou hast given up thou shalt receive a hundredfold, even in this present life.

Farewell, and seek after perseverance, which alone gaineth a crown.

XXXV. SAINT BERNARD AND POPE INNOCENT II.

[1138 ...... 47.]

To the Lord Pope Innocent, concerning the Church of Langres.

Whilst I was still at Rome there chanced to come there the Lord Archbishop of Lyon. And with him there came Robert, Dean of the Church of Langres, and Olric, Canon, requesting that it might be permitted to them and to the chapter of Langres to elect for themselves a Bishop. A mandate indeed they had received from the Lord Pope, in no way to take the matter in hand, unless with the counsel of religious men. This, when they desired and sought through me to obtain, I said, "This be far from me, unless I know and am sure that ye intend to choose a good and fit person." They replied that their purpose and intention should depend upon my advice, and that they would not do other than I should counsel them. They pledged themselves to this. But as I was not sufficiently assured of their good faith, the Archbishop supported their request, promising firmly the same thing. And he added, that if the clergy should endeavour to do differently, whatever other course they might adopt should not in the least be confirmed by him, or deemed as settled. My Lord the Chancellor also testified to the like resolve. Not fully contented I went even into the presence of my Lord the Pope, so that by his favour and authority what had been agreed upon between us should be confirmed. A mutual conference of ourselves was held daily as to the election to be carried out, and from the many names mention of which by them was made, two were at length selected, as to whom no one of us would at all dissent, and would be pleased with whichever of them should be chosen. And so the Lord Pope gave forth that what we should be agreed upon should be unchangeably observed, and the Archbishop and the clergy also promised steadfast accordance with this. Upon their departure I stayed several days in the city, whence, when I was able to obtain permission to return from my Lord, I started upon the road to my brethren.

While crossing the Alps I found that the day was drawing nigh on which would be consecrated to the bishopric of Langres, a man, of whom would that I had heard better and more honourable things. But I will not tell what I unwillingly heard. By not a few religious, who had met

me for the sake of saluting me, I was persuaded
to turn aside to Lyon, so that I might prevent
if it were possible the doing of the nefarious deed.
For I, because of the weakness and weariness of
my body, had resolved to go by a shorter way,
especially as, I confess, I did not give clear
credence to the rumours I heard. And so, ac-
cepting the counsel of the religious, I took the
road towards Lyon, and on arriving there saw
that arrangements were being made, just as I
had heard. The solemnities—not festal, but of ill
omen—were being prepared for. Yet the Dean,
and the greater part, if I am not mistaken, of the
Canons of Lyon, protested incessantly and openly.
The shameful and lamentable rumour had filled
the city and was increasing and gathering strength
in all directions.

What could I do? I conferred with the Archbishop, and with reverence, upon the agreement
which he had made, and upon the counsel to
which he had given acceptance, and he denied
nothing as to what had been decided upon. But
referring to the cause of his straying from his
promise, he spoke of the Duke's son as having
kept himself aloof from what had been promised.
Lest he should be disturbed, he himself had
fallen away from his former purpose, in the
interests, forsooth, of peace.

XXXVI. SAINT BERNARD AND POPE INNOCENT II.

[1139 ...... 48.]

To the Lord Pope Innocent, in behalf of Alberone, Archbishop of Trèves.

Boldly I speak because faithfully I love.   For that love is not sincere in which the tiniest doubt retaineth a taint of suspicion.   The grievances of the Lord of Trèves are not his alone, but are common to many, and especially to those who love you with a sincere affection.   The one voice of all amongst us who in authority have faithful care of the people, asserteth that justice is perishing in the Church, that the keys of the Church have been abolished, that episcopal authority is altogether trampled on, whilst no one of the bishops cometh forward to avenge wrongs, or to chastise unlawful deeds, not even in his own diocese.   The cause of this they declare to be you and the Roman Court.   The things that have been put right by them, they say you destroy: what they have rightly destroyed you set up again.   Whatever shameful and contentious folk, whether from amongst the clergy, or even such as have been driven out of monasteries, run to you, when they return, declare with triumphant gestures that they have secured as a protector one from whom they ought rather to have received punishment. Your friends are confounded, the faithful feel themselves treated with contumely, the bishops everywhere come in for reproach and disgrace, inasmuch as their righteous judgments are despised, and your authority also is very much slurred.

But these are they who are zealous for your honour, who for your peace and exaltation toil faithfully indeed, yet I fear not with success. Why do you cut down your own power? Why do you trample down your own strength? With what intent do you beat back the faithful weapons fighting for you? The church of St Gingulphus weeping deploreth her desolation at Toul, and there is no one to console her. For who would oppose himself to the lofty arm, to the rushing torrent, to the will of the highest power? The Blessed Paul at Verdun lamenteth that he hath to endure the same violence, the Archbishop not being able to defend him from the wildness of the monks, who are indeed too fully strengthened by apostolic help as though they were not wild enough by themselves.

With such sacrifices God is not propitiated, His anger is not appeased, His grace is not conciliated, His mercy is not called forth. For these and like things the anger of the Lord is not yet turned aside, but His arm is stretched out still. God also is indeed angry with separatists; but He in no wise looketh with favour upon Catholics. The Church in Metz, as is well known to you, is endangered by the serious contentions of the bishop and clergy. As to which, what it shall please you to decide, you must know; but there is no peace yet, nor is it hoped for in the near future.

See what you can do as to these bishoprics— these of Metz and Toul—since, as I confess is the truth, they seem to be without bishops. Would that they were without tyrants! When such are defended, supported, honoured, favoured, many wonder very much, and are scandalized,—many, who know that in the conduct and in the lives of such, there are those things that should rather be utterly condemned and execrated, and ought to be, not only in bishops, but even in any laymen whatsoever.

These things, indeed, it hath shamed me to write, and it hath not been fitting for you to hear. Be it so, that while no one accuseth them they cannot be deposed; yet, ought those whom rumour everywhere accuseth, to be in such special intimacy with the Apostolic See as to be in receipt of its favours or be singled out for advancement?

*   *   *

Who will secure justice for me from you? If I had a judge to whom I could take you, I would at once show you (as one in great sorrow I am speaking) what you have deserved. The tribunal of Christ indeed standeth out before us; but be it far from me to summon you to that. I, who (if it were necessary for you, and possible for me) would wish rather with all my strength to stand there myself and respond for you. And so I return to him to whom it is given in the present time to judge the world, that is to yourself. You I summon to yourself. Judge ye between me and yourself.

XXXVII. SAINT BERNARD AND ABBOT BALDWIN OF RIETI.

To Baldwin, Abbot of the Monastery of Rieti.

Teaching, Doing, Praying.

The letter which thou hast sent is fragrant
with thine affection. It arouseth mine. I grieve
that I am not able to write back just as I am
moved. Nor will I linger over excuses, knowing
that I am speaking to one who knoweth me.
Do not thou by the brevity of my letter, judge
of mine affection, which no speech, even by its
lengthiness, would be able to set forth. The
troublesomeness of the things that demand mine
attention cause me to write with few words,
but not that I should love thee little. As a
mother loveth her only son, so did I love thee,
when thou wast close at my side, delighting mine
heart. Let me love thee in thine absence, lest
I seem to have loved the solace that was mine
from thee—the solace of thy presence—and not
thyself.

Do thou take care to be found a faithful and

123

prudent servant. To thy fellow-servants communicate the celestial bread without partiality, and pray without ceasing. Do not thou make unmeaning excuses, as if by reason of thy newness in thy work, or of thine inexperience; for perchance, thou mayest think so, or thou mayest pretend so to think. For neither is a fruitless modesty pleasing, nor is a humility beyond what is fitting, commendable. Therefore attend to thy duty. Dispel bashful feelings by the thought of thine office. Act as a teacher should. Prepare to act in accordance with the only talent confided to thee, without care for aught else. If thou hast received much, give much; but if little, give that little. For who in the least is not faithful will not be so in the greatest.

Remember also to give to thy voice the note of valour. "What is that?" dost thou ask? Let deeds harmonise with thy words, or rather thy words with thy deeds; so that thy care may be rather to act than to teach. It is a most beautiful and most salutary order of life, that the burden which thou layest on others to be borne, thou shouldest first bear thyself. Thus from thyself thou mayest learn to control others. Therefore, on these two commands—as to speech, forsooth, and as to example—understand that there depend the highest efficiency of thine office and

the freedom of thy conscience from care. Still
if thou art wise thou wilt add also a third, zeal in
prayer, in correspondence so to speak with that
threefold repetition in the Gospel as to feeding
the sheep. In this thou wilt recognize that the
sacrament of that trinity is in no way frustrated
by thee, if thou dost feed by speech, if thou dost
feed by example, if thou dost feed also by the
fruit of holy prayer. Thus there abideth these
three—speech, example, prayer, but the greatest
of these is prayer. For although as I have said,
the valour of speech is manifested in action, yet
prayer imparteth grace and efficacy to both
action and speech.

XXXVIII. SAINT BERNARD
AND KING ROGER OF SICILY.

[1139 ...... 48.]

To Roger, King of Sicily.

Far and wide hath the report of your magnificence spread over the earth. For what shores are there that the glory of your name hath not reached unto? But listen to the advice of one who loveth you. Study, as far as in you lieth, to attribute this same glory to Him from whom it cometh, if you do not wish to lose it, or to be destroyed assuredly by it. This will be your endeavour if you open the eye of your discretion upon those whom the widespread renown of your magnificence calleth from afar, and if you reach out your hand not so much to the grasping as to the needy. Blessed is he who considereth, not the grasping, but the needy and the poor. The poor one who asketh reluctantly, receiveth with modesty, and receiving giveth glory to his Father who is in the heavens. But when from the mouth of the needy God's own glory from your own gift will be so faithfully ascribed, that fount of glory must flow for you with stream more bounteous, and by no means with doubtful movement, since He loveth those who love Him, and glorifieth those who glorify Him, as verily he who soweth in the midst of blessings shall reap blessings. Wherefore I entreat you to turn your eyes upon the bearer of this letter, whom not greed hath drawn towards your royal presence, but necessity hath driven,—necessity, I say, not his own, but that of his brethren the many faithful servants of God, by whom forsooth he hath been sent. Hear patiently what they have to suffer patiently; hear and have compassion; for if with them you suffer, with them you shall reign. And to reign with such is not to be despised, even by a king. For theirs is the kingdom of the heavens who have despised the worldly life.

*　　　*　　　*

If you seek me, lo! here I am, and my children, whom God hath given to me. For my humility is reported to have found favour with His Majesty the King so that he seeketh to see me. And who am I that I should hide from my view the good pleasure of the king? I hasten, and to him by whom I was sought, I say: "Lo! here I am, not with the body's weak presence, but in my children. For who shall separate me from them? I shall follow them wheresoever they shall go; and if they shall dwell in farthest sea, they will not be divided from me. Thou hast, O king, the light of mine eyes; thou hast mine heart, and my soul. What if the least of me is absent? I speak of this little body, this worthless possession, which my will would set free, but necessity keepeth hold of. It is not able to follow the soul in its flight, since it is weak and the sepulchre is almost alone left for it. But why should this be a care? Do not wonder, O king! I would choose rather to wander from the body, than to send them away, if God alone had not failed to be the cause. Receive them as strangers and pilgrims, but nevertheless as fellow-citizens with the saints, and of the household of God. It is not enough to call them citizens; they are kings. For theirs is the kingdom of the heavens, by the right and merit of poverty."

*   *   *

You have what you asked for; you have done what you promised. Those whom at your word we sent forth to you have been welcomed with royal generosity. You have met them with bread, you have led them to a cool retreat, you have placed them on a lofty hill, that they may eat the fruit of the fields, that they may draw honey out of the rock, and oil from the hardest stone: that they may draw butter and milk from the herd, and gather figs, and procure the flour of wheat, and drink the purest juice of the grape. And these indeed are earthly things, but they buy heavenly things. Such is the pathway to the stars; such sacrifices God looketh upon with favour. For the kingdom of the heavens is theirs who in the land of the living will have been able to render to an earthly king, in return for these good things of earth, eternal life and glory.

I have sent you Master Bruno, formerly for many days my companion, but now the father of many souls who in Christ are rejoicing, but in earthly things are needy. Let him also have experience of the generous hand of the king. What you do for him you do for me: since what is lacking to him is required from me. But because my purse is sufficient only for a little, I have taken care to induce the monk, poor for the merit of Christ, to trust to yours, which seemeth to be somewhat weightier than mine.

XXXIX. SAINT BERNARD AND THE ABBOT OF ST AUBIN.

[1140 ...... 49.]

To the Abbot of St Aubin.

Thou art unknown to me by face, but not by
fame, and I not a little congratulate myself that
I have this valued knowledge. For I confess that
by it thou hast so found an entrance into mine
heart, that taken up as I am with many things,
that most delightful impression of thyself, my
dearest brother, often with ease beareth me away
from them all, so that I linger upon it with gladness and rest in it with sweetness. But the more
I welcome the thought of thee, the more eagerly
I long for thy presence to my sight. But when
will that be, if ever? Still, if not before, certainly in the city of our God, if here indeed we
have no continuing city, but are seeking that one.
There, there, I shall see thee, and mine heart will
rejoice. In the meanwhile I shall not the less
be delighted and rejoice in the things I am told
about thee, hoping and expecting that there will

be left for me a sight of thy bodily presence in the day of the Lord, that my joy may be full. Add, I entreat thee, to those good things which from thee and concerning thee are constantly coming to me, thy prayers and the prayers of thy brethren for myself, my dearest and most-longed for father.

XL. SAINT BERNARD AND BER-
NARD OF PISA, AFTERWARDS
POPE EUGENIUS III.

[1140 ...... 49.]

From Abbot Bernard of St Anastasius, near
Rome, to Saint Bernard.
To his venerable Lord and dearly loved Father,
Abbot of Clairvaux, his son Bernard sendeth
greeting.

As often as that day of misery and calamity
on which I was torn from thy consoling presence,
cometh back to my memory, I am more disposed
to weep than to write. If the outflow of my words
were as great as that of my tears, thou wouldest
easily understand my forlornness. As my mind
applieth itself to meditation, and my hand to
writing, my grief is renewed. That bitterest
bitterness of mine returneth to me as I write.
So doth the sad picture of that day, in which
my foolish self was raised to dignity, and I am
disturbed. I do not blame, my Lord, thy deed,
or the intention of thy deed, to which thou

132

art believed to have been directed by the finger of God, but I bewail somewhat my sadness. For lo! after I was withdrawn from the sight of thine eyes, my life was worn away in grief, and my days in mourning. To me is woe; because I have lost the pattern to which I was being conformed, the mirror in which I saw what I might be, the light of mine eyes. No longer soundeth that sweet voice in mine ears, no longer doth that face, which was wont to blush at my failings, present itself to mine eyes. Wherefore, my Lord, am I frustrated in my hope? Why am I defrauded of my desire? My life hath been broken off as a thread in the weaving.

I did not sufficiently understand when I was in Clairvaux that I was in a place of happiness amid the trees of Paradise, and therefore I esteemed as nothing that land so delightful. What, my Lord, what in me attracted thy consideration, that thou didst place me as a leader and teacher of men, that thou didst appoint me as a ruler over thy people? Was it my doings in the world? But they were worthless. Was it my life in the monastery? But that was lagging and lukewarm. Wherefore when I was little in mine own eyes have I been made the head of a tribe of Israel? Wherefore, when I was not cleansed from secret sins, hast thou not spared

133

thy servant from undertaking the burden of those of others? What can a man do, whom sorrow for the past, the burden of the present, and fear for the future, press down upon? At the summit of my grief, at the height of my misery, I presume to speak thus to thee alone, my Lord so longed for, because I received my wound from one not thought of as an enemy.

XLI. SAINT BERNARD AND POPE INNOCENT II.

[1141 ...... 50.]

To his most dear Father and Lord, Innocent, by the grace of God supreme Pontiff, Bernard, called Abbot of Clairvaux, sendeth greeting.

Many are called, but few are chosen; and thus there is no great argument for having trust in a matter of doubtful import, or thinking it worthy of commendation, because it is commended by many. The Archbishop of York, as to whom I have very often written to your Holiness, hath come to you—a man who hath not chosen God for his helper, but hath trusted in the multitude of his riches. His cause is a faulty one, and a weak one; and as I learn from the witness of truthful men, from the sole of the foot to the crown of the head there is no wholesomeness in it. What then? What seeketh a man devoid of justice, from the enquirer after justice, from the guardian of equity? Doth he think that he will be able to swallow up justice in the Curia, as he hath swallowed it in England? He hath swallowed up a stream, and maketh no marvel of it, and hath confidence that the Jordan will now flow into his mouth. Lo! he hath come along with many, whom he hath won over to himself, both by entreaties and by bribes. One alone hath evaded him, to make known to you the truth. He would be quite alone, but right hath not left him to loneliness. What then will the Vicar of Peter do in this cause submitted to him? What but that which Peter did with him who thought that a gift of God could be bought with money? I speak not thus from myself alone, but according to the testimony of those who are led by the Spirit of God.

*   *   *

These whom you see before you are simple, and upright, and men who fear God. And now in the spirit of God they have ascended to the sight of your glory, to gaze upon justice and to gain her aid. Turn your eyes, I pray you, upon the poor men in their weariness, since not without cause they come to you from afar, not heeding the great distances by land, the peril of the sea, the snows of the Alps, or the cost of the journey, even though they are poor. Let my Lord, then, give a thought to them, that neither the fraud nor the ambition of anyone prevail so as to render useless their toils, especially as they are seeking not things of their own, but the things of Jesus Christ. For not even an enemy, I deem, can suspect them of being led on in this matter by any private love or hate, but by the fear alone of God. So if any one is of God, let him join himself to them. If the unfruitful tree shall henceforth encumber the ground, whose fault shall I call it, save the fault of him who holdeth the axe?

XLII. SAINT BERNARD AND THE QUEEN OF JERUSALEM.

[1142 ...... 51.]

To Melisendis, Queen of Jerusalem.

Men have heard that I have favour with you; and many on the eve of setting out for Jerusalem seek to be commended by me to your Excellency. Amongst whom is this young kinsman of mine, a youth, as they say, strenuous in arms, gentle in manners. And I rejoice that he at a fitting time hath chosen to fight for God rather than for the world. Accordingly do as is your wont, and may it be well with him because of myself, as it hath been with all other kinsfolk of mine who have been able through me to make themselves known to you.

As to other matters, take heed lest the pleasure of the flesh, and the glory which is of time alone, bar for you the road to the heavenly kingdom. For what profit is it to reign for a few days upon earth, and to be deprived of the eternal kingdom of the heavens?   But I trust in the Lord that you

will do better, and if the testimony which my
dear Uncle Andrew beareth concerning you is
true,—and I in him have much faith—you will,
with God's mercy, reign both here and in eternity.
On pilgrims, on those in need, and especially on
those in prison, bestow care; since for such sacrifices God granteth His favour.

Write to me more frequently; since it will be
of no disadvantage to you, and will be helpful to
me, if I shall know more fully and more certainly
your spiritual state and your efforts for good.

---

*To Melisendis, Queen of Jerusalem, Daughter of
King Baldwin, and Wife of King Fulk.
For the most illustrious Queen of Jerusalem,
Melisendis, Bernard, Abbot of Clairvaux,
wisheth health, and desireth that she may
find grace in the sight of God.*

Among the manifold cares and occupations of
a royal court, it would seem to me to be unfitting
to write, if I had regard only for the glory of thy
realm, thy power, and thy noble lineage. All
these things are present to the eyes of men; and
they who have them not, envy those who have
them and think the one happy who is possessed

of them. But what is the blessedness in possessing those things, which all wither away quickly like grass, and fall rapidly as the flower of grass? They are good; but they are fleeting, they are changeable, they soon disappear, they are perishable, because their goodness is of the flesh. And furthermore of the flesh, and of its good things, it hath been said: "All flesh is grass, and all its glory is as the flower of grass." Therefore it doth not behove me to shrink much from writing to thee because of these things, as they have a favour which is deceitful, and a beauty that is vain.

Receive, therefore, what in few words, I say. Receive my counsel, brief, but useful, from a distant land,—counsel from which, as from a small seed, an abundant harvest shall arise in the future. Receive, I say, counsel from the hand of a friend, who seeketh not his own advantage but thine honour. No one indeed can be to thee more faithful as to counsel than he who loveth, not what he might receive of thine, but thyself alone. The king thy husband being dead, and the young king being as yet little fit to bear the burdens of a realm and to devote himself to the duties of a king, the eyes of all look towards thee, and upon thee the whole weight of reigning resteth.

THE QUEEN OF JERUSALEM

There is need that thou shouldest put thy
hand to brave deeds, and in womanly fashion
act as a man, doing those things which must be
done in the spirit of counsel and strength. So
prudently and discreetly it behoveth thee to
arrange all things, that all who shall behold thee
shall deem thee to be a king rather than a queen,
lest perchance amongst the nations they say:
"Where is the King of Jerusalem?" But thou
wilt say: "I am not sufficient for these things.
For these things are great: they are beyond my
strength, and beyond my knowledge. These
duties are the duties of a man; but I am only
a woman, weak in body, fickle in heart, neither
foreseeing in counsel, nor accustomed to toils of
office." I know, my daughter, I know. These
things are great; but this also I know, that
though wonderful are the waves of the sea, the
Lord on high is also wonderful. These things
are great, but great is our Lord, and great is
His power.

XLIII. SAINT BERNARD AND KING LOUIS VII.

[1142 ...... 51.]

To Louis, King of France.

I fear I have not troubled about you without cause.   For, too quickly and too lightly you have turned away—as is clear—from the good and wholesome counsel which you had accepted, and have hurried back, as I fear, by reason of I know not what diabolical advice, to the former evils which you rightly bewailed with still recent lamentations having perpetrated.   From whom, unless from the devil, shall I say hath come this advice, by which it happeneth that fires are added to fires, slaughters to slaughters, and the renewed cry of the poor, and the shrieks of those in shackles and the blood of the slain, sound in the ears of the Father of the fatherless and the Judge of widows? Clearly with these sacrifices the ancient enemy of our race may be delighted, since he is a murderer from the beginning.

You listen not to words of peace, nor do you

142

keep your compacts, nor do you consent to wise counsels; but, by what decree of God I know not, you so turn for yourself all things into their opposites, that you deem shame as honour and honour as shame; you fear what is free from danger, you despise what should be feared; you love those who hate you, you have hate for those who wish to love you. For those who press you to repeat your former malice against such as do not deserve it, seek not, in so doing, your honour, but their own advantage; yet not indeed their own advantage, but to give pleasure to the devil.

In the slaughter of men, in the burning of houses, in the destruction of churches, in the driving out of the poor, you join yourself with robbers and plunderers, as though you were not sufficiently able to do mischief by yourself. I tell you, you will not be long unpunished if you continue to do such things as these. And therefore, my Lord King, I advise you with a friendly purpose, and I counsel you faithfully to desist quickly from this malignity, if perchance you may by penitence and humility stay the hand of Him who is preparing to smite you. I speak harshly, because I fear harsher things are in store for you; but remember what hath been said, "Better are the wounds of a friend than the false kisses of an enemy."

143

XLIV. SAINT BERNARD AND THE ROMAN CURIA.

[1145 ...... 54.]

The Abbot of Clairvaux marvelleth that Bernard,
Abbot of St Anastasius, should be drawn
away from quietness and solitude, and have
thrust upon him the care of the whole Church.
He feareth that the man accustomed to a calm
life, and little practised in carrying on weighty
affairs, may not be equal to so great a burden.
So that he prayeth that the new Pope may be
sustained by the faithful assistance of the
Cardinals.

To the Lords, and Reverend Fathers, all the
Cardinals and Bishops who are of the Curia,
the son of their Holinesses sendeth greeting.

May God forgive you! What have ye done?
A man who was buried ye have recalled amongst
men. One who had fled from cares and crowds,
ye have once more involved in cares, ye have
once more made mingle with crowds. Crucified
to the world, through you he now liveth again in

the world. He who had chosen to be in lowliness
in the house of his God, ye have elected to be
lord of all. Why have ye confounded the counsel
of the needy? Why have ye disturbed the resolve
of one who was poor and indigent and smitten in
heart? He was running well. Why have ye
thrown a hedge across his road, turned aside
his paths, baffled his footsteps? As though he
should be going down from Jerusalem, and not
rather ascending from Jericho, he will fall among
thieves. He who had vigorously shaken himself
free from the wiles of the evil one, from the be-
guilements of the flesh, and from the attractiveness of the glory of the world, had nevertheless
not the power to escape from your hands. Did
he therefore flee from Pisa that he might be
attracted to Rome? Did he who withdrew from
being second in authority in one Church, seek
indeed the supreme authority over the whole
Church?

What reason or counsel induced you, when
the supreme Pontiff was dead, to suddenly rush
upon a rustic, to lay hands on him in his retreat,
and wresting from his hands axe, trowel, or hoe,
bear him off to a palace, raise him to a throne,
clothe him with purple and fine linen, gird him
with sword to smite with vengeance nations, to
rebuke peoples, to bind their kings in chains, and

their nobles with links of iron? Was there not amongst you a man wise and experienced whom such responsibilities would have better suited? Laughable, certainly, it seemeth, that a man lowly and tattered should be raised to preside over princes, to rule bishops, to dispose of kingdoms and empires. Laughable is it, or miraculous? Assuredly one of these it is. I deny not, I do not distrust, that even this may have been the work of God, who alone worketh great marvels, especially when I incessantly hear from the mouths of many that such hath been done by the Lord. And I am not unmindful of the Scripture which telleth how many have formerly by the will of God been called from a private or even from a rustic life, to reign over the people. Did He not choose David His servant in such a way, and take him from the sheepfolds? So, I say, it may have been by God's good pleasure with our Eugenius.

Still I am not quite assured since my son is of a yielding disposition, and of a tender modesty accustomed rather to quietness and restfulness than to dealing with the things that are without; and it is to be feared that he will not perform the duties of his Apostolate with becoming authority. What think ye now will be the mental attitude of a man who seeth himself drawn from the depths of spiritual contemplation, and from the friendly solitude of the heart, into the midst of activities, and into unwonted and unattractive duties? Unless the Lord uphold him with His hand, he will unfailingly be crushed and oppressed by a burden, strange and over-weighty —a burden which seemeth, as they say, a formidable one for the shoulders of a giant, or even for those of an angel. But because the change hath now been wrought, and, as many say, wrought by the Lord, it is for you, dearly beloved, by your fervent zeal and your faithful endeavours, to bestow fostering and anxious care upon what hath been accomplished with the help of your own hands. If therefore there be any consolation in you, if there be any power of love in the Lord, if any tender mercy, if any inward compassion, assist him and toil with him in the work to which through you he hath been called by the Lord. Whatsoever things are true, whatsoever things are pure, whatsoever things are just, whatsoever things are holy, whatsoever things are lovely, whatsoever things are of good report, suggest them to him, press them upon him, do them with him ; and the God of peace shall be with you.

XLV. SAINT BERNARD AND POPE EUGENIUS III.

[1145 ...... 54.]

To Pope Eugenius III.

*Bernard congratulateth Eugenius, lately raised
to the Pontificate, and condoleth with him.
He encourageth him to bravely advance upon
his apostolic duties, so that he may respond to
the expectations entertained of him by many.
To his beloved Father and Lord, by the grace of
God supreme Pontiff, Bernard, called Abbot
of Clairvaux, sendeth greeting.*

Tidings have reached our land, and have gone
round us all, as to what the Lord hath done for
you. Hitherto I have restrained my pen, and
have pondered in silence. For I looked for a
letter from you, and hoped to be forestalled by
you in a blessing of sweetness. I was hoping,
too, for some faithful man, who would come from
your side, and who would narrate to me in due

148

order, of everything that had been done, how it had been accomplished, and of its true import. I was looking to see if perchance one of my sons should return to soothe a father's grief, and say, "Joseph, thy son, is alive, and is ruler over all the land of Egypt." Hence it is that this letter is not of free will, but of necessity, and is extorted by the prayers of friends, to whom I cannot deny what little remaineth of my life. But as I have once begun, I will speak to my lord. For I dare not call you now my son, because the son hath been changed into father, and the father into son. He who came after me hath been preferred before me; but I am not envious, because what was lacking in me, I trust that I possess in him who came not only after me but also through me. For if you will permit me to say it, I have in a way begotten you through the Gospel. What then is my hope, and my joy, and my crown of glorying? Is it not you before God? A wise son is indeed the glory of his father. From now however you will not be called son, but a new name which the mouth of the Lord hath spoken will be given you. My son Bernard by a joyful and beneficent translation hath been promoted to be my father Eugenius.

Since this change hath taken place in you, it now remaineth that the bride of your Lord, who hath been entrusted to your care, may be changed for the better. Claim nothing of hers as your own : but for her, if there shall be need, you ought even to give your life. If Christ hath sent you, you will think that you have not come to be ministered unto, but to minister unto others, and to minister not only your own substance, but even your very soul.

Having such confidence in you as she seemeth not to have had for a long time past in your predecessors, the whole Church of the Saints everywhere rightly rejoiceth and glorieth in the Lord. May I not too rejoice with those who do rejoice? Shall I not be one of the number of those who are glad? I rejoiced, but I confess, with trembling ; I rejoiced, but in the midst of my rejoicing fear and trembling came upon me. I have laid aside the name of father, but not a father's fear, not a father's anxiety, not a father's affection, not a father's heart. I look at the height, and I fear a fall. I look at the height of your dignity, and I behold the abyss that lieth below. I see the loftiness of your honour, and I shudder at the danger nigh at hand, because of that which is written, " Man when he is in honour hath not understanding." His honour hath absorbed his understanding.

And indeed you had chosen to be lowly in the

house of God, and to sit in the lowest room at
His feast, but it hath pleased Him who invited
you to say, "Friend, go up higher." And as you
have ascended on high, be not high-minded, but
fear. You have forsooth obtained a higher place,
but not a safer one—a loftier one, but not a more
secure one. Terrible indeed, terrible is that place.
The place in which you stand is holy ground. It
is the place of Peter. It is the place of the Prince
of the Apostles, where his feet have stood. It is
the place of him whom the Lord appointed lord
of His house, and prince of all His possessions.
And if perchance you should turn aside from the
way of the Lord, Peter was buried in the same
place, that he may be for a testimony against
you.

*   *   *

To Pope Eugenius.

In all thy doings remember that thou art but
a man, and let the fear of Him who taketh away
the breath of princes be ever before thine eyes.
How many Roman Pontiffs hast thou in a short
time seen with thine eyes, who are now dead!
Let these very predecessors of thine warn thee of
thine own most certain and most speedy departure
hence ; and let the short time of their domination

tell thee of the fewness of thine own days. Therefore with continual meditation amid the allurements of thy transitory glory, remember the days thou hast left behind not far away; since those whom thou hast succeeded in thy paternal see thou shalt without doubt follow on to death.

*　　*　　*

[1146 ...... 55.]

To Pope Eugenius, on behalf of the Abbot of Cluny.

It seemeth unwise to write to thee for the lord of Cluny, and to appear as though I wished to be a patron to him whom all desire to have as patron for themselves. Yet, I write, although for his sake it is not necessary, to satisfy my affection for him—I say, my affection, not another's. For as I cannot be with him in person, I thus follow my friend as he journeyeth. Who shall separate us? Not the height of the Alps, not the cold of the snows, not the length of the road. And now I am present with him, helping with these words of mine. Apart from me he shall never be.

Honour the man as a truly honourable member of the body of Christ. A vessel he is, if I am

152

not mistaken, full of grace and truth, abounding with very many excellences. Send him back with joy, to make joyful very many by his return. Honour him with ampler favour as worthily he may be favoured, and so that from the fulness of his grace, when he shall return, we may receive of it. Assuredly if he shall desire anything in the name of the Lord Jesus, he ought not to meet with any difficulty from thee. For if thou knowest it not, he it is who extendeth his hand to the poor of our Order; he it is who from the possessions of his church, freely and often bestoweth gifts of food, as much as he can with the acquiescence of his brethren.

XLVI. SAINT BERNARD AND
THE FRENCH CLERGY.

[1146 ...... 55.]

*To the Clergy and People of Eastern France.
For the very dear Lords and Fathers, Arch-
bishops, Bishops, and all the Clergy and
People of Eastern France and Bavaria.
Bernard, called Abbot of Clairvaux, desireth
that they may abound in the spirit of strength.*

A word from me to you concerning the service
of Christ in whom is our salvation. The earth of
a certainty is shaken and trembleth, because the
God of heaven hath begun to lose His own land.
His own, I say, in which the Word was seen, and
for more than thirty years lived as a man with
men; His, which He illumined with marvels,
which He made sacred with His own blood:
in which appeared the first flowers of the Resur-
rection. And now, at the call of our sins, the
enemies of the Cross have lifted up their sacrilegious heads, striking down with the sword the

154

dwellers in the land of promise. They soon, if there be no one to resist them, will be rushing into the very city of the living God, be overturning the sanctuaries of our redemption, be polluting the holy places — places sacred to the sinless Lamb—making them purple with blood. O grief! with sacrilegious mouth they gape at the very shrine of the Christian faith, and strive to invade and tread upon the very bed in which for us our Life slept in death.

What are ye doing, O brave men? What are ye doing, servants of the Cross?... For the wicked enemy to become possessed of the Holy of Holies would be an inconsolable grief to all ages to come, because an irrecoverable loss, an infinite shame to this most impious generation, an everlasting reproach.

*   *   *

Since therefore your country is fruitful in brave men, and is known to abound in robust youth, so that your praise resoundeth everywhere, and the renown of your bravery hath filled the whole world, gird ye yourselves manfully, and take up arms of happy promise in zeal for the Christian name.

Brave knight, battle-loving hero, thou mayest now take up weapons without danger. It is glory to conquer; it is gain to die. Take the sign of the Cross, and thou shalt obtain pardon for every sin which thou shalt confess with a contrite heart.

But it is needful to warn you, dearest brethren, that if there is anyone amongst you longing to be foremost in the fight, and who should wish by an expedition of his own to forestall the kingdom's army, let him by no means be so venturesome. And if he pretend to have been sent by us, it is not true. Or if he produce letters as given by us, they are entirely false, or obtained by guile. Let men of bravery, and leaders of skill be chosen, and let the army of the Lord start all at the same time, so that it may have strength everywhere and sustain no violence from anyone soever. For there was in a former expedition, before Jerusalem was captured, a certain man, Peter by name, of whom ye, if I am not in error, have often heard mention. He placing himself alone in command of the people who had entrusted themselves to him, led them into dangers so great, that there were none, or at least very few, who did not perish, either by hunger or by the sword. Let not the like happen to you, by your doing as did they. May God, who is blessed for ever, avert such danger from you. Amen.

XLVII. SAINT BERNARD AND THE ABBESS HILDEGARDE.

[1146 ...... 55.]

*To the Abbess Hildegarde, his beloved daughter
in Christ, Bernard sendeth greeting, and for
her wisheth health and all that the prayers
of a sinner can obtain.*

I congratulate thee on the grace of God which
is in thee, and counsel thee that thou receive it as
grace, and that thou endeavour to respond with
entire affection of humility and devotion, knowing
that God resisteth the proud but giveth grace to
the humble.

But where there is interior wisdom and the
unction which teacheth of all things, what am
I able to teach or advise?   For thou art said to
investigate heavenly secrets, and to have an insight into things which are beyond human reach,
by the light of the Holy Spirit.   Whence I pray
the more and humbly entreat that thou wilt have
me in memory before God, and those too who
are joined with me in spiritual brotherhood.

XLVIII. ST BERNARD AND COUNT HILDEFONS.

[1147 ...... 56.]

Of how many evils have we heard and known, which the heretic Henry hath done or doeth daily in the Church of God? He as a rapacious wolf goeth about in your land, under the clothing of a sheep; but as the Lord hath said, by his fruits we know him. There are churches without people, people without priests, priests treated with irreverence, and, in truth, Christians without Christ. Churches are thought no more of than synagogues; the sanctuary of God is denied to be holy; sacraments are not thought of as sacred; festival days are deprived of their solemnities. Men die in their sins, souls are hurried away everywhere to the awful tribunal, alas! neither reconciled by penitence nor fortified by holy communion. From the children of Christians the life of Christ is kept away by the denial of the grace of baptism, and they are not permitted to draw nigh unto salvation, though the Saviour lovingly crieth unto them, "Suffer the little children to come unto Me."

XLIX. SAINT BERNARD AND
SAINT MALACHI.

[1148 ...... 57.]

Life of Saint Malachi, Archbishop of Armagh.
A.D. 1094—A.D. 1148.

Our Malachi, born in Ireland in the midst of
a barbarous people was there brought up and
instructed. But from his barbaric native land
he drew nothing and retained nothing more than
fishes retain of the maternal salt of the sea. How
did such a wild uncultured land produce for us
one so truly gentle, one so refined a fellow-citizen
of the saints and of the household of God! He
who produceth honey out of the rock, oil from
the hardest stone, hath Himself done this!

     *   *   *

When he began to devote himself to his
sacred duties the man of God found that he had
been placed not over men but over beasts. He
had never hitherto experienced such unparalleled
barbarism, never before found any so grotesque

in their manners, so revolting in their rites, so
impious in their faith, so uncontrolled by law,
so headstrong as to discipline, so unclean in life.
They were Christians in name, but Pagans in
reality. They would not give tithes or firstfruits;
they would not enter into lawful wedlock, or
make confessions; neither were any to be found
who would either seek for or perform penance.
Of ministers of the altar there were very few.
But what need was there for more? There were
not any of them who performed their duties
amongst the worthless people around them. In
the churches there was not heard the voice
either of preacher or of chorister. What was
the athlete of the Lord to do? Was he to give
up the struggle disgracefully, or to keep it up
with danger? But he who knew himself to be a
shepherd and not a hireling chose to stay and
not to flee, prepared, if there should be need,
to give his life for the sheep. And although all
were wolves and not sheep, the intrepid shepherd stood in the midst of the wolves, resolved
to try by every kind of appeal to transform the
wolves into sheep. He admonished publicly;
he pleaded secretly; he wept over them one by
one; he met them sometimes severely, sometimes
gently, as it seemed best to do in each case. If
by such means he made little progress he cer-

tainly made for them the offering of a contrite and humble heart. How many nights did he spend wakefully, stretching out his hands in prayer! And when the people were unwilling to come to church, he would run after them through streets and squares, and going round the city would seek breathlessly for anyone whom he might gain for Christ.

*   *   *

Malachi got to know of the plot (to attack him), and entering into a church close by, with uplifted hands he prayed unto the Lord. And behold clouds and thick darkness, and a darksome storm from clouds of brass, turned day into night. Lightning also and thunder, and frightful blasts of a hurricane, as though announcing the last day, all the elements telling of the approach of death.... And that thou mayest know, reader, that it was the prayer of Malachi that shook the elements, the tempest cut off those only who had sought after his soul; the darksome whirlwind caught into its rush only those who had prepared works of darkness. Even the prince who had stood forth as the instigator of wrong-doing, struck by lightning, was killed with three others; and they were consorts in death who had been sharers in crime. On the following day their half-burnt bodies were found, putrid, lodged in the branches of trees, whither the wind in its fury had blown them. Other three, half-living, were found; all the others were scattered all around. But those who had been with Malachi, although they had been very close to the spot, the tempest had in nowise touched, and had brought them no harm. In this we have an experience of the truth of the saying, "The prayer of the righteous pierceth the skies"

*   *   *

In this very city of York there came to him a man noble in secular rank, Wallen by name, then Prior of Kirkham, a priory of regular brothers; now a true monk, and a father of monks, in the monastery of our Order at Melrose. With humility and devotion Wallen commended himself to the prayers of Malachi. He noticing that the Bishop had many companions and few horses—for besides servants and other clerics, there were with him five priests, and only three horses—offered him his own horse, on which he himself was wont to ride, though he troubled himself that the horse was rather restive. And he adds : "I would have given it with the more pleasure, if it had been better; but if you will deign, take him with you whithersoever you will." "And I," said the Bishop, "accept it the more willingly the more you pronounce it of little worth, for whatever such precious goodwill hath given to me, cannot be deemed by me to be of little value." And turning to his own retinue, he saith: "Saddle him for me, for he will be suitable enough, and will be sufficient for a long time." Which having been done, he mounted the horse, and though he at first felt him indeed to be wild and restless, after a while found that the creature underwent a wonderful change, and trotted on very comfortably and easily. And this best and most valuable of palfreys did not fail him right up to the ninth year afterwards, in which year he himself died. And what was very strange, he began from being nearly black to change to white, and not long after scarcely a horse could be found of a whiter hue.

*   *   *

To me also in this life it was given to see this man (Archbishop Malachi) and at the sight of him, and in listening to his words, I was refreshed and delighted as in all kind of riches. And I in my turn, sinner though I was, found grace in his sight, from that time and onwards, even to his death, for he deigned to turn aside to Clairvaux, and when he saw the brethren, he was touched to the heart, and they too were not a little edified by his presence and by his speech. And taking the place and ourselves into his

affection, and indeed gathering us into his intimate embrace, he bade us farewell, and departed,
to cross over the Alps (to Rome where he was
received by the Pope, Innocent II, with kindness
and hospitality).

*   *   *

Though from the west he came, he who
visited us (this visit being a third one, in 1148,
ten years after the first one) came to us truly as
the dayspring from on high. O how did he as
a radiant sun add to the brightness of our
Clairvaux! What a joyful festive day brightened
upon us at his coming! This is a day which the
Lord hath made, for us to rejoice and be glad
in it! How quickly did I, trembling and weak
though I was, leap towards him, as soon as he
drew nigh! How joyfully I saluted him! With
what joyfulness did I embrace him as a favour
sent me from heaven itself! With what eager
countenance and heart, did I lead thee into our
beloved house! What festive days afterwards
did I pass with thee, but how few! How did he
in his turn comport himself towards us? Indeed,
our pilgrim showed himself smiling, affable, and
incredibly gracious to all. How good and how
cheerfully he acted as a guest with ourselves, to
see whom he had come from the ends of the
earth, not to hear a Solomon, but to let us hear

one! We heard at last his wisdom; we were favoured with his presence; we shall ever keep his presence with us in our memories.

Already four or five days had flown by, when lo! on the solemn festival of Saint Luke the Evangelist, as the Holy Communion was being celebrated in the monastery with impressive devotion, he was seized with fever, and had to rest on his couch. We, all, gathered around him. Grief drove away our joy, still grief subdued, since for a while the fever seemed to be but slight. You might see the brothers running this way and that, eager to obtain something for him, eager to give something to him. To whom was it not sweet to see him? To whom was it not sweeter to minister to him? All were anxious to be of service to him, to procure medicine, to apply fomentations, to urge him to take food oftener. To whom he said: "This is unnecessary; but for your love I do whatsoever ye enjoin." He in truth knew that the time of his departure was approaching.

When the monks, who had come with him, besought him earnestly not to lose hope of life, for no sign of death showed itself in him, he said: "It must be that this year Malachi must leave the body. Lo! the day draweth nigh, which, as ye well know, I have ever wished should be the day of my removal hence. I know in whom I have trusted, and am sure I shall not be deprived of the rest of my desire, as I have already secured a part. He who in His mercy hath led me to the place which I sought, will not refuse to me the end which I have equally desired. As to this body, here is my resting-place. As to my soul, the Lord will provide, who maketh safe those who hope in Him."

The day of which he spoke was not far off. In the meanwhile he requested that he might be anointed with the sacred oil. Going out of the convent of the brethren that it might be solemnly administered, he would not consent that the brethren should ascend to him; he himself descended to them. He rested himself in the sun-room of the upper house. He is anointed, and having received the Viaticum, and then commending himself to the prayers of the brethren, and commending them to God, he returneth to his bed. He had walked down to the sun-room, and he would do no other than walk back again to his lofty chamber. He said that death was at the door. But who would believe that he was about to die? Himself only and God could know. His face did not seem very pale or emaciated, his brow was not wrinkled, his eyes were not sunk, his nostrils had not be-

166

come thin, his lips were not drawn, nor his teeth faulty, his neck was not shrunken or slender, his shoulders not bent, and his flesh not wasted on the rest of his frame. Such was the grace of his body, and such the glory of his countenance, that not even in death could they disappear. Such he was as long as he lived. Such he was also when dead; he was very like to one living.

The Festival of All Saints is with us—a bright solemnity everywhere. But according to the old saying, "Music in mourning is a tale out of season." We are present; we sing, or rather we are invited to do so. Weeping we sing, and singing we weep. Malachi though he singeth not, yet doth not weep. Why should he weep, who is drawing nigh unto joy? Grief is left unto us, who are being left by him. Malachi alone keepeth the Festival. For what is not possible with the body he doeth with the soul. While the instrument of the body is failing him, while the tongue is silent, while the voice's office is ceasing, he is still able to keep the solemnity with the song of his soul. Why should not the saint keep the solemnity, the saint who is being led to the solemnity of the saints? He displayeth to them what soon will be due to himself. A little longer and he is one of them.

In the twilight of the evening, when already

the solemnities of the day are completed by us, Malachi draweth nigh, not to the twilight but to the dawn. Is it not dawn for him, to whom the night advanceth, and yet day draweth nearer? The fever so increaseth upon him that now everyone beginneth to despair of his life, each draweth back his former judgment. No one hath now any doubt that Malachi's word as to himself is true. We are summoned. We present ourselves. He raising his eyes on them who are standing around, saith: "With desire I have desired to eat this passover with you. I give thanks to God, that I have not been deprived of my desire." Seest thou a man safe in death, and yet not dead, yet sure of life? And it is not wonderful. Seeing the night to be the night which he had expected, and in it day dawning for himself; as though triumphing over the night, he seemeth to defy the darkness, and in a way to speak thus: "Now I will not say, Perchance the darkness will overwhelm me, since this night is my illumination in my delights." And gently consoling us, he saith: "Think of me; I, if it shall be permitted me, will not be forgetful of you. But it will be permitted. I have trusted in God, and all things are possible to one who trusteth in Him. I have loved God; I have loved you; and love never dieth." And looking up towards heaven he saith: "O God, in Thy name keep these, but also all who through my word and ministry have devoted themselves to Thy service." Then placing his hands on each one, and blessing them all, he biddeth them retire to rest, because his hour hath not yet come.

We go; we return about midnight; for in that hour the light to lighten in darkness is announced. The house is filled; the whole congregation is present. Many abbots also have gathered together. With psalms and hymns and spiritual songs we follow our friend as he is journeying towards his Father's home. In the fifty-fourth year of his age, in the place, and at the time, which he had chosen and predicted, Malachi, the Bishop and Legate of the Holy Apostolic See, is as it were taken by angels from our hands, and falleth asleep happily in the Lord. Truly he falleth asleep. A placid countenance is the index of a happy transit. And indeed the eyes of all are fixed upon him; yet there is no one who is able to notice when he passeth away. When dead he is thought to be living. When living he is thought to be dead. There is no moment of time falling between his living and dying to divide the one from the other. There is the same brightness of countenance,

169

the same serenity which was wont to appear in him as he slept. You would say that death had borne away nothing of these, but had rather added very much to them. He is not changed, but he hath changed all of us. In a marvellous manner the grief and sobs of all are suddenly hushed. Sorrow is changed into joy; song chaseth away lamentation. He is carried out, voices are lifted up towards heaven; he is borne into the oratory on the shoulders of abbots. Faith hath conquered. Affection is triumphant.

And in real truth what reason have we for unrestrained lamentation over Malachi, as if his death were not precious, as if it were not rather a sleep and not death, as if the portal of death were not also the portal of life? Malachi our friend sleepeth, and shall I bewail? If the Lord hath given sleep to His beloved, and such a sleep, in which is the inheritance of God, the reward of the Son, which of these seemeth to tell me to weep? Shall I shed tears for him who hath escaped from tears? He exulteth in joy, he triumpheth, he entereth into the joy of his Lord; and over him shall I mourn? I desire these things for myself, I have no envy for him because he hath them.

In the meantime his funeral rites are prepared for; Holy Communion is celebrated for him; all things are carried out in accustomed way with highest devotion.

The solemnities having been reverently performed in that very chapel of the Holy Mary, the Mother of the Lord, in which Malachi himself had ever taken delight, he is carried out for burial, in the year of the Lord 1148, on the 2nd of November.

Thine, Good Jesus, is the treasure which was entrusted to us. We have kept it to be given back to Thee when Thou dost deem it well to ask for its return. We pray Thee only that he may not depart hence without his companions, but that he whom we have had for our guest, we may have for our leader, so that with Thee and with him we may hereafter reign for ever and ever. Amen.

L. SAINT BERNARD AND THE DUCHESS OF BURGUNDY.

To the Duchess of Burgundy.

The special friendliness of your Grace towards
ourselves, poor though we are, hath been so
widely recognised, that whosoever thinketh that
he hath your Grace hostile to himself, trusteth
to return to your favour by no one more easily
than by myself.

Hence it is that when I was at Dijon a while
ago, Hugo de Bèse pressed me with many prayers
to soften towards himself your indignation which
he had deserved; and that you should, for the
love of God, and out of friendship for ourselves,
proffer your consent to his son's marriage, which
though not pleasing to you, but, as he thinketh,
advantageous to himself, he had unalterably resolved to arrange for. Concerning this matter
he hath now again, both by his own appeals, and
by the entreaties of his friends, been dinning his
demands into our ears.

As to worldly advantages we do not much

172

care; but yet, because the matter, as he himself saith, seemeth to be so hedged in with difficulty, that except with violation of what he hath sworn, he can in no way oppose the marriage, we have thought it fitting to intimate this to you, since great ought to be the usefulness of that which should be preferred to the consistent fidelity of one who is a Christian man and also devoted to your service. For he cannot be a man faithless to his word and at the same time remain faithful to his liege Lady. Moreover also we see not only no gain coming to you, but indeed much danger befalling you, if those on whom God hath bestowed approval on their being joined together, should haply be disturbed by you.

May the Lord, upon you and your children, most noble Lady, in Christ to me so dear, bestow His grace. Dispense your corn amongst the poor of Christ, that in eternity you may with usury receive it back again.

LI. SAINT BERNARD AND
POPE EUGENIUS III.

[1150 ...... 59.]

To his very dear Father and Lord, Eugenius, by
the Grace of God Supreme Pontiff, Brother
Bernard, called Abbot of Clairvaux, sendeth
greeting.

If any vessel fit for the great house of the
Great King is held in honour in our Church of
France; if any one is as a faithful David coming
in and going out at the Lord's command, in my
judgment such a one is the Venerable Abbot of
St Denys. I know him indeed as a man who
in temporal things is faithful and prudent, and
in spiritual things fervent and humble, and in
both without blame. In the presence of Caesar
he is as one of the court of Rome. In the
presence of God he is as one of the Court of
Heaven. I ask and pray that the messages of so
great a man may be received by you graciously,
and as it becometh you, and as he himself is
altogether worthy I beseech you to write back
to him words good and friendly, full of familiarity
and affection, full of favour and grace; for indeed
to love and honour very specially his person, is
to do great honour to your own ministry.

LII. SAINT BERNARD AND
ABBOT SUGER.

[1151 ...... 60.]

*For his dearest and intimate friend Suger, by
the grace of God Abbot of St Denys, Brother
Bernard desireth the glory which is from
within, and the grace which cometh from
on high.*

That peace awaiteth thee which passeth all
understanding. The righteous await for thee to
behold thee receive thy reward. The joy of thy
Lord awaiteth thee. And I, my dearest friend,
am anxiously desiring to see thee, that the
blessing of one about to die may come upon me.
And since no one can choose the way he would
traverse, I dare not, as I am not certain, promise
to come of a surety ; but though I do not yet see
how I can come, I do quite what I can. Perchance I may come : perchance I may not come.
But whichever of these it may be, I have loved
thee from the very first, and shall love thee
onwards unceasingly. I say, with faithfulness,

SAINT BERNARD AND ABBOT SUGER

I cannot lose so loved a friend, even at the last.
To me he doth not die, but he goeth on before,
he to whose soul mine own hath clung and hath
been cemented with a hold which will not be
unloosed, and with a chain which cannot be
broken. But remember me when thou shalt
have gone whither thou goest before me, so that
it may be granted to me to follow thee and to
come to thee. Until then in no way think that
thy sweet memory may depart from me, though
thy presence is withdrawn from thy grieving
friends. God is however able to give thee to
us in answer to our prayers, and to preserve thee
for us who have need of thee; of this we must
assuredly have no doubt.

LIII. SAINT BERNARD AND
COUNT THEOBALD.

[1151 ..... 60.]

You know that I love you, but how much so
God knoweth better than you. That I also am
beloved of you I do not doubt, and that you
love me for God's sake I doubt not. If I should
offend Him then you ought not to love me, as
then God would not be with me. For who am
I that so great a prince should care for me who
am so small, except so long as you believe that
God is in me? Therefore, my offending Him
would perchance not be well for you. But it is
far from doubtful that I shall offend Him if I
do what you ask. For ecclesiastical honours
and dignities I do not forget are due to those
who both resolve and are able to administer
them worthily for God. Furthermore that such
should be obtained for your youthful son by my
prayers or by yours is neither just for you nor
so for me. For it is permitted neither to any
one, nor even to an adult, to hold several honours

in several churches except, indeed, by dispensation, by reason of the Church's great need, or for special usefulness to individuals. On account of which if this letter seemeth to you harsh and it pleaseth you to fulfil what you are contemplating, spare me in the matter, for you are well able, if I am not deceived, to obtain what is sought for through yourself or through other friends of yours. And thus not the less you will accomplish what you wish, without my having sinned. Certainly to our little William I wish well in all things, but before all things that God should be with him. Hence it is that I wish not that he should have aught contrary to God, so that God should not be with him. But if any one else wish otherwise I am unwilling that he should obtain what is desired through me, lest I also lose God. Still when anything shall arise which he is able to have in accordance with God's will, I will prove myself a friend and if need be, will not deny mine aid. Before a lover of righteousness there is no need for me to toilsomely make much excuse for doing that which is righteous. Do you also to your Countess, through these things which I have written, have me excused. Farewell.

LIV. SAINT BERNARD AND
POPE EUGENIUS III.

[1151 ...... 60.]

*To Pope Eugenius, after the death of the
Bishop of Auxerre.*

I now mention something as to which I
before would not have been silent, if it had
been known to me, as it now is. There is here
a man who hath made Israel to sin. I am
speaking with reference to the holy bishop, who
when he was at the point of death, and was a
little dull and dazed, this man caused to die
almost intestate. For while he hath bestowed
nothing or almost nothing upon the poor and
the churches, to his nephew according to the
flesh, youthful, a secular and of little usefulness,
he hath left almost all that he had acquired for
the episcopal table, and this he did at the
prompting and at the urgent request of this
nephew Stephen. They say that he hath left
him seven churches, and tithes, and the meadows

in the bishop's own woods; and further, which is a shame for all religion, from his moveables the vessels that are of gold and his own equipages, and since these could scarcely suffice for the accomplishment of a journey, they also say that in order that he may come to you for the confirmation of these bequests, he hath even left directions for the equipages of a monastery to be given up to him. Although some think that the bishop knew nothing of these donations, but that Stephen drew up and obtained his signature to whatever he chose, and this is credible. For last year also when the bishop was, as was thought, in the very turn of death, they caused him to bestow a certain church on this same nephew; which gift afterwards when he was convalescent, as I have got to know of a certainty, he did not in the least remember to have made. Who, indeed, would believe that a man, holy and spiritual, would, if he were not bereft of wisdom, if he were of sound mind, have made such a testament? Who is there having fullest familiarity with worldly doings, would have said that this was the testament of a priest? Is such the disposition of a sober and spiritual man, of one who adjudicateth about all things, and himself is judged by no one? If the matter remaineth unaltered, who in heaven or on earth, will not adjudge him as deserving of blame?

Do thou, then, O servant of God, who holdest the sword of Peter, cut away this reproachful confusion from religion, this scandal from the Church, this crime from the individual, and from all spiritual men who loved him with an affection spiritual and not carnal, and prove thine own heart bitterness and grief. Arise, Phinehas, stand and appease, that the shaking may be stayed —stand, I say, inflexible against flesh and blood, by which battering-ram the sons of this world without doubt are endeavouring to make the wall of thy constancy totter. It will be true affection towards the uncle, if over an affair of this kind you show yourself pitiless towards the nephew.

LV. SAINT BERNARD AND THE QUEEN OF JERUSALEM.

[1153 ...... 62.]

To the Queen of Jerusalem.

For his beloved daughter in Christ, Melisendis, Queen of Jerusalem, Bernard, called Abbot of Clairvaux, desireth mercy from God his Saviour.

I marvel that now for a long time I have not seen any letter of thine, and have not received thy wonted greetings, as if I had forgotten thine ancient affection towards me, which I have in many things proved. I have heard, I confess, I know not what strange rumours of thee, which although I have not believed them undoubtingly I have yet grieved that whether by truth or by falsehood thy repute should be in any way tarnished. My dear Uncle Andrew, whom I cannot in anything disbelieve, hath stepped in, putting down in his letter to me better tidings, that forsooth thou bearest thyself peacefully and gently, that thou rulest thyself and thy people wisely, and with the counsel of the wise; that thou lovest thy brethren of the Temple, and hast friendly intercourse with them; that thou dost, according to the wisdom given to thee by God, encounter with forethought and wisdom, making use of salutary counsels and help, the dangers threatening thy land. Such doings certainly become a brave woman, a humble widow, a Queen of high rank.

For neither because thou art a Queen, is it a disgrace to thee to be a widow; such, if thou didst wish thou mightest not be. I think that it is also not less a glory to thee especially among Christians, to live as a widow, than as a Queen. The one is of succession; the other is of virtue. The one is thine by right of birth; the other is a gift of God. The one hath been obtained by happy descent; the other by brave resolve. Twofold is the honour; the one according to the world, the other according to God; but each from God. And let not to thee seem small the honour of widowhood, as to which the Apostle saith: "Honour widows who are widows indeed."

Remember that thou art a Queen, whose deeds of worth cannot lie unworthily beneath a bushel. They are on a candlestick, that they may appear unto all. Remember that thou art a widow, of whom now it is required not that she may desire to please her husband, but that she may please God alone. When thou thinkest of thy dignity, remember also thy widowhood, since thou canst not be a good Queen if thou art not a good widow.

May the Lord bless thee out of Sion, my daughter exalted in the Lord, and worthy of all veneration.

LVI. SAINT BERNARD AND HIS UNCLE ANDREW.

[1153 ...... 62.]

To his Uncle Andrew, Knight Templar.

Thy letter which thou didst send last, found me on a bed of sickness. I received it with stretched-out hands. I read it gladly, and gladly did I read it again ; but more gladly would I see thee. I have read in it thy desire to see me. I have read also of thy fear as to the danger threatening the land which the Lord honoured with His presence, and threatening the city which He dedicated with His blood. Woe to our princes ! In the land of the Lord they have done no good. In their own to which they returned so swiftly they are working incredible mischief. Powerful they are to do evil ; but good they are unable to do. But we trust that the Lord will not drive back His people, and will not desert His heritage. Moreover the right hand of the Lord shall show forth strength, and His arm will render assistance ; so that all may know that it is good to trust in the Lord rather than to look for succour to princes.

Thou desirest to see me; and, so thou dost write, on me it dependeth whether thy desire shall be accomplished. For thou sayest thou dost wait for my instruction as to this. And what shall I say to thee? I both desire that thou shouldest come, and fear lest thou shouldest do so. Thus placed between wishing and not-wishing I am hindered by both; and what I shall choose, I know not. By seeing thee I should satisfy thy desire and mine own equally; but am I not rather to trust to the general opinion concerning thee, by which thou art proclaimed to be so necessary to the Holy Land, that from thine absence therefrom desolation not slight is believed to be threatening it? Therefore I dare not command thee, and yet I do wish that I may see thee before I die. Thou thyself art better able to see and to know, if thou canst in any way come without injury and without trouble to that land. And it might be that thy coming would not be altogether useless. Perchance, by the help of God, there might not be wanting some who would accompany thee on thy return, to render succour to the Church of God, since thou art known to all and art beloved by all.

One thing I say, if thou shouldest come, not to delay, lest perchance thou shouldest come, and find me not. For already I feel myself gliding away, and think I have not long to be upon earth. Would that to me were granted, the Lord being willing, to be refreshed by thy sweet and loving presence even for a little while, before I go hence!

I have written to the Queen, as thou didst wish, and rejoice at the good testimony thou dost proffer concerning her. I salute through thee in the Lord, the Master and all thy Brethren of the Temple, and those of the Hospital also. Likewise I salute all the saints with whom thou mayest have opportunity of speaking, and commend myself to their prayers. Be my messenger to them. Our Gerard, who for a while consorted with us in our house, and now, as I hear, hath been made a bishop, I also salute most devotedly, with great affection.

LVII. TO ARNOLD OF CHAR-
TRES, ABBOT OF BONNEVAL.

The last letter written by Saint Bernard.

[1153 ...... 62.]

I have received thy loving message with
loving welcome, but not in the midst of delight.
For what delight can there be when bitter suffering claimeth all for itself? Sleep hath left me.
So that the kindness of unconsciousness never
enableth pain to quit my senses....And in all
this—that nothing may be hidden from an anxious
friend as to the state of his friend—as to the
inward man, I may say that the spirit is willing
though the flesh is weak. Pray to the Saviour,
who willeth not the death of a sinner, that He
will not put off my departure, now so seasonable,
but will keep watch over me as I pass away.
Take care to fortify by thy prayers one who is
void of merit, that he who lieth in wait may not
be able to find where he may fix his tooth and
inflict a wound. These words I have written,
in mine affliction, that by the hand well known
to thee, thou mayest recognise my love for thee.
But I should like to have answered a letter from
thee rather than to have written first.

LVIII. SAINT BERNARD ON THE MYSTERY OF THE SOUL.

A Meditation.

Not to the contemplation of things without will I devote myself, but I will meditate upon what I find within me, and from things of lowly import within me I will ascend to those above me ; so that I may be able to know whence I came, and whither I go ; what I am, and from whom I am, and thus from knowledge of myself may be able to come to the knowledge of God. For the more I advance in knowledge of myself, the more do I progress towards a knowledge of God.

Accordingly I find in my soul three things, by which I retain the thought of God, contemplate Him, and long for Him. These three are— memory, discernment, and will or love. By memory I am minded of God ; by discernment I see Him ; by the will I love and clasp Him. When I keep God in my thoughts, in my memory I find Him, and in that memory I receive a

delight from Him and find a delight in Him
according to what He Himself deigneth to grant
to me. By my discernment I see what God is
in Himself, what He is in angels, what in saints,
what in other beings, what in men. In Himself
He is immeasurable because He is beginning
and end, beginning without beginning, end without end. From myself I understand how immeasurable, how incomprehensible, God is, since
I am not able to understand myself whom He
hath made. In the angels, He is One to be
yearned for and loved, because their delight is
ever to behold Him. In the saints, He is full
of delight, because in Him those happy ones continually rejoice. In other beings, He is worthy
of admiration, in that He createth all things by
His power, ruleth all things by His wisdom, and
by His loving forethought provideth for them all.
In men, He is such as to call forth love, because
He is their God, and they are His people. He
dwelleth in them as in His own temple. He
hath no disdain for any single one, or for any
community or society. Whosoever hath Him
in his thoughts, and discerneth Him, and loveth
Him, is with Him.

*   *   *

Happy is that soul with whom God findeth
His resting place, and in whom as in a tabernacle

He is at rest. Happy he who is able to say:
" He who hath created me hath also found rest
in my tabernacle." To him the rest of heaven
will not be denied.

Why then do we go out of ourselves, and in
things outside us seek God who is with us, if
only we desire to be with Him? In truth He
is with us and in us ; but, as yet, only by faith,
until we are worthy to see Him in clear vision.
"We know," saith the Apostle, "that Christ
dwelleth in our hearts by faith," because Christ
is in our faith, faith is in our soul, our soul is
within us.

By faith, then, I think of God as my Creator,
I adore Him as my Redeemer, I look for Him as
my Saviour. I believe that I see Him in all His
creatures, that I have Him in myself, and, which
is unspeakably more joyful and happy than all
else, that I know Him as He is in Himself. For
to know the Father and the Son with the Holy
Spirit, is life eternal, perfect bliss, highest delight.
Eye hath not seen, nor hath ear heard, nor hath
it entered into the heart of man to conceive what
brightness, what sweetness, and what joy will
be reserved for us in that vision when we shall
see God face to face—when we shall see Him
who is the Light of all that have received
enlightenment, the Rest of all who have been

His soldiers, the Country of all who return from
earth, the Life of all who dwell in life, the Crown
of all who have triumphed.

*   *   *

As a star glittering in the sky runneth swiftly
and falleth suddenly, and as a spark from a fire
is speedily extinguished and reduced to ash, so
swiftly do we see life come to an end. For
whilst man lingereth on earth in gladness and
joy, and thinketh that he hath yet long to live,
and setteth his mind for a long time hence upon
many things that he will do, he is suddenly
snatched away by death, and his soul is borne
from his body with startling abruptness.

*   *   *

O my soul, ennobled by being in the image
of God, honoured by bearing His likeness, united
to Him by faith, dowried with the breath of His
life, redeemed by divine sufferings, accounted
as of angelic worth, capable of blessedness, heir
of all goodness, sharer in divine wisdom, what
hast thou to do with the body whence come to
thee so many ills? On account of thy flesh it
is that sins not thine own are imputed to thee,
and thine own righteous deeds are thought of
as only filthy rags, and thou thyself art reduced
to nothing and art accounted as void of everything. For the flesh with which thou art in so

192

close an alliance is nothing but froth, vested only
with a fragile grace. In a while it will be but
a wretched decaying frame. How much soever
it is cared for, it is ever only flesh.

*　　*　　*

When thou shalt have entered the church for
prayer or praise, leave outside the tumult of
wavering thoughts, and be inwardly forgetful of
all care as to outer matters, so that thou mayest
be free to devote thyself to God alone. For it
is not possible that there should at any time talk
with God, one who at the same time is also
silently chatting with the whole world. Give
attention therefore to Him who giveth attention
to thee. Listen to Him as He speaketh to thee,
that He Himself may hear thee when thou speakest to Him. It will thus happen that if thou
assistest at the utterance of divine praises with
due reverence and thoughtfulness, if thou heark-
enest intently and diligently to every word of
Holy Scripture, thou wilt hear God speak to thee.
Not that I say that I do these things ; but I wish
to do them ; I grieve at not having done them ;
I am vexed when I do them not. But do thou
to whom greater grace is granted, with vows and
devout prayer turn towards thyself the merciful
ears of the Lord ; with tears and sighs beseech
Him to look with clemency on thy wanderings

from faithfulness, and with spiritual beings praise and glorify Him in all His works. For nothing more pleaseth the citizens on high, nothing giveth more joy to the Heavenly King.

*   *   *

Whosoever with prayer and diligent devotion is watchful towards the spiritual world, will depart hence safely, and be received into that world with great joy. Wherever therefore thou shalt be, pray secretly within thyself. If thou shalt be far from a house of prayer, give not thyself trouble to seek for one, for thou thyself art a sanctuary designed for prayer. If thou shalt be in bed, or in any other place, pray there; thy temple is there. By frequent prayer, by bending the body in lowly devotion, the mind is exalted towards God. For as there is no moment in which man doth not experience and enjoy the goodness and mercy of God, so there ought to be no moment in which he ought not to have God present in his thoughts.

*   *   *

Deal with thyself as with a temple of God, inasmuch as there is that within thee which is like unto God. The highest honour indeed that can be rendered to God is to venerate Him and to imitate Him. Thou wilt imitate Him if thou art devout and full of piety. For a devout and

194

pious soul is a holy temple of God, and a righteous heart is His altar. Thou wilt venerate Him if thou art merciful, as He Himself is merciful to all. This is an acceptable offering to God, to do good unto all for God's sake. Do all things as a son of God, that thou mayest be worthy in the sight of Him who hath deigned to call thee His son. In all things that thou doest, know that God is present with thee. Take care therefore that no evil have a delight for thee, so that no sight or thought of it may take thee from God. Neither speak nor do that which is wrong, even though it is pleasant, and by no word or sign offend God, who being present everywhere seeth whatsoever thou doest.

*　　*　　*

God speaketh to me, and I to Him, in a Psalm ; and yet when I say the Psalm, I heed not what the Psalm telleth me ! Therefore I do a great wrong in His sight, when I beseech Him that He will hear my prayer, which as I give utterance to it I do not hear myself. I entreat Him that He will think of me ; but I regard neither myself nor Him. Nay, what is worse, turning over corrupt and evil thoughts in mine heart, I thrust a dreadful offensiveness into His presence.

*　　*　　*

Nothing in me is more changeable than mine heart, which as often as it deserteth me and wandereth through perverse resolves, so often doth it offend God. Mine heart—my vain, wandering, unsteady heart—whilst it is led on by its own will, and is without divine counsel, is not able to remain attached even to itself, but is more restless than everything that is restless, is distracted by an infinity of things, and strayeth hither and thither along numberless paths. And whilst in divers ways it seeketh rest, it findeth none; but in the midst of toil it remaineth wretched, in the midst of rest it remaineth dull and thoughtless. It is not in harmony with itself; it is indeed at discord with itself. It recoileth from itself, it passeth from one resolve to another, it changeth its decisions, it reareth up something new, it destroyeth the old, it rebuildeth what it hath destroyed, the same things again and again in one fashion or another it disarrangeth and setteth in order again, because it wisheth and doth not wish, and never remaineth in the same mood. For as a windmill it revolveth rapidly, and taketh in everything, and grindeth whatever is placed in it; but if nothing is put within it, it grindeth away and setteth itself in a blaze. Thus mine heart is ever in motion, and is never at rest; but whether

I sleep or am awake, it dreameth and pondereth over whatever cometh before it. And as sand if placed in a mill, destroyeth it, as pitch defileth it, as chaff choketh it, so bitter thoughts disturb mine heart, unclean thoughts stain it, vain thoughts disquiet and weary it. Thus mine heart careth not for future joy, and seeketh not divine aid; it departeth from the love of heavenly things, and is filled with a fondness for earthly things. And when it falleth away from heavenly treasure and becometh wrapped up in that which is earthly, vanity absorbeth, curiosity beguileth, greed allureth, pleasure seduceth, luxury corrupteth, envy distracteth, anger disturbeth, sadness tormenteth that heart; and thus the sport of wretched fancies, it becometh enslaved to every vice, since it hath dismissed God, who alone would have been its unfailing support.

Amid many things the soul wandereth bewildered, and seeketh hither and thither where it may rest, and findeth nothing that yieldeth satisfaction, until it returneth to God. It is led from one distracting thought to another distracting thought, it strayeth here and there, giving itself up to various pursuits and fancies, so that at length it exhausteth the variety of the things it hath concerned itself with, which however are not of a sort to satisfy and content it.

197

Thus when divine grace is withdrawn doth the
heart's misery lead it downwards.

*　　*　　*

I am not able to conceal my sins, since
wherever I go my conscience is with me, bearing
with itself whatsoever I have placed in it, whether
good or evil. Whatsoever it hath received to be
kept, it keepeth during the lifetime, it restoreth
when this life is ended. If I do wrongly, conscience is present with me; but if I seem to do
well, and am therefore elated, still conscience is
present. It is present with me in life; it followeth
me when I am dead. Everywhere there is with
me and inseparable from me, either approval or
shame, according to the sort of burden laid upon
my conscience. Thus, in mine own house, as it
were, and in the midst of mine household, I have
accusers, witnesses, judges, and bestowers of
punishment. Conscience accuseth me, memory
witnesseth, reason judgeth, pleasure is my prison,
fear my gaoler, sinful delight my torment. For
as many as have been the evil delights so many
will be the dread torments as punishment, for
we are punished there, where our very delights
spring from.

*　　*　　*

O the loving-kindness of Christ! O unlooked
for salvation for sinners! So free, so nigh, is

198

the love of God ; so amazing His tender mercy,
so unexpected His condescension, so invincible
His clemency, that whosoever calleth upon Him,
He heareth that one, since He is merciful.   O
how great is the mercy of God ! how unspeakable
the change wrought by the hand of the Highest !
Yesterday thou wast in darkness ; to-day thou
art in the splendour of light.   Yesterday thou
wast in the mouth of the lion ; to-day in the
hand of the Mediator.   Yesterday thou wast in
the gate of hell ; to-day amid the delights of
Paradise.......Thy toil shall end in rest, thy sorrow
in joy, and after the shadows of this life thou
shalt see the rising of a new dawn, thou shalt
see the mid-day Sun of Righteousness, the Bridegroom and His mystic Bride, the one Lord of
Glory, who liveth and reigneth for ever and
ever.   Amen.

LIX. SAINT BERNARD AND
SAINT VICTOR.

A Meditation.

Let us study henceforth to be conformed to
his ways, to whom in his marvellous doings we
are not able to be like, though we wish so to
be. Let us emulate his sober living, his devout
affection. Let us emulate his courtesy of spirit,
his chasteness of body, his guardianship of the
lips, his purity of mind. Let us place restraint
on our anger and keep check on our tongues ;
let us sleep more sparingly, pray more frequently,
and in psalms and hymns and spiritual songs
more often with one another commune. Let
us join the nights to the days and fill them with
divine praises. Let us emulate him in the better
gifts. Let us learn from him, because he was
meek and lowly in heart. Let us emulate him,
I say, because he was generous towards the poor,
cheerful towards guests, patient with sinners,
kind towards all. For such is better.

In these things we shall be impressed by the

beauty of him, by the glory of whose doings we are but humbled. The marvellous doings cause us to rejoice. They will edify us and prompt us to advance.

*　　*　　*

The veteran soldier resteth now in due sweetness and security ; secure indeed as to himself, but anxious for us. For not even with the decaying flesh could he at the same time put off the bowels of kindness, and he doth not so clothe himself with the state of glory as that he should at the same time clothe himself with forgetfulness of our misery and of his own tender mercy. It is not a land of forgetfulness, that which the soul of Victor inhabiteth ; it is not a land of toil, in which he becometh wholly absorbed ; it is not indeed earth, but heaven. Will a celestial habitation harden the souls of those whom it receiveth, or deprive them of memory, or despoil them of kindness? Brothers, the breadth of heaven dilateth, not narroweth, hearts ; exhilarateth minds, not alienateth them from reason ; it doth not contract the affections, but expandeth them. In the light of God the memory is made bright and is not obscured ; in the light of God is learnt what was not known, and what is known is not unlearnt. Those supernal spirits, who inhabit heaven from the beginning, do they because they dwell in heaven, despise the earth? Do they not rather visit it and frequent it? Because they always behold the face of the Father, doth affection disappear from their ministry? Are they not rather ministering spirits, sent forth to minister unto those who are heirs of salvation? What then? Shall angels run to and fro, and succour men, and shall they who are from ourselves, lose all knowledge of us, and not know how to have sympathy with us in the things which they themselves have suffered? Shall they be unconscious of our sorrows, who nevertheless have known them? Shall they who have come out of great tribulation have no recognition of those who are still in tribulation?

Hail, therefore, mighty athlete, sweet patron, faithful advocate, arise to our help, that both we may rejoice in our deliverance, and that thou mayest boast in the fulness of victory.

O Victor Jesus, we praise Thee in our Victor, because we know that Thou hast conquered in him. Grant to him, O most loving Jesus, so to glory concerning his victory in Thee, that he may not enter into forgetfulness of us. Son of God, permit him ever in Thy presence to be mindful of us.

LX. SAINT BERNARD ON "THE NAME OF JESUS."

Arid is every food of the soul if it is not mingled with this oil. Insipid is it if not seasoned with this salt. If thou writest, thy letter is not sweet to me unless I read in it of Jesus. If thou dost preach or dost hold converse, what thou sayest is not pleasant to me unless there sound in it Jesus. Jesus is honey in the mouth, melody in the ear, a song of delight in the heart. He is also a healing portion. Is any one of you sad? Let Jesus enter into the heart of such one, and thence leap to his lips; and lo! at the rising light of His name, every cloud fleeth away, and brightness returneth.

LXI. SAINT BERNARD. ADVENT MEDITATIONS.

The Lord's Spiritual Advent.

As our Lord came once in visible form on earth to work out the salvation of men, so He cometh now spiritually and invisibly to save individual souls. And that thou mayest know that this spiritual coming is mystical and hidden from view, He saith, Under His shadow shall we live among the nations.

It doth not behove thee, O man, to cross the seas, to pierce the clouds. It is not needful for thee even to pass over the Alps. A way not long is pointed out to thee, I say. To meet thy God thou must go simply to thyself. For His word is nigh thee, in thy mouth, and in thine heart. Seek a refuge in sorrow of heart, and in confession of the lips, so that thou mayest at least quit the defilement of a conscience depraved ; for it would be an indignity to the Author of purity for Him to have to enter there. Thus

have I spoken of that coming, by which He
designeth to enlighten individual souls by His
invisible presence.

The Body and the Soul.

O body, thou art able to hinder the salvation
of the soul, but art not able to work out thine
own. As far as thou hinderest its restoration,
thou hinderest thine own. Thou art not able
to be restored until God seeth His own image
reformed in thine indwelling soul. Thou hast
a noble guest, O flesh, an exceedingly noble one,
and thine entire salvation dependeth on its
salvation. Give honour to a guest so great.
Thou indeed abidest in thine own region; but
thy soul as a pilgrim and an exile is a guest with
thee. I ask thee, what peasant, if perchance any
one noble and of great influence wisheth to tarry
with him, as a guest, will not willingly rest himself in a corner of his house, or on its steps, or
in the midst of its very ashes, so that he may
give up the more fitting place, as will be worthy,
to his guest? Do thou also likewise. Thine own
wrongs or troubles think nothing of, only that
thy guest may remain with thee duly honoured.
There is honour for thyself in that thou, for the
sake of thy guest, submittest to dishonour.

And lest perchance thou shouldest despise

205

or think slightingly of thy guest, by reason of his
seeming to thee only a wanderer and a stranger,
give heed diligently to the things wherewith his
presence enricheth thee. For he it is who giveth
sight to the eyes, and hearing to the ears. He
it is who supplieth voice to the tongue, taste to
the palate, motion to all thy members. If there
is in thee any life, any sensation, any comeliness,
see in such the beneficence of this guest. His
departure at last proveth what his presence conferred. For when the soul departeth, at once
the tongue will be silent, the eyes will see nothing,
the ears will be deaf, all the body will become
rigid, the face will become pale. In a short time,
also, the whole frame will become putrid and
foul, and all its comeliness will be turned to
corruption. Wherefore then dost thou for the
sake of any fleeting pleasure, sadden and injure
that guest, when, except through him, thou
wouldest not be able to experience that pleasure
at all? If as an exile and as one by reason of
enmities cast away from the face of the Lord,
he conferreth upon thee such great things, how
great things will he, if reconciled, bestow on
thee? Do not, O body, hinder that reconciliation, since from such, great is the glory that is
prepared for thee. Patiently, yea, even willingly,
submit thyself to every yoke; shrink from nothing

which seemeth to thee likely to help on that
reconciliation. Say to thy guest : "Because the
Lord will remember thee and restore thee to thine
earliest exaltation, do thou likewise remember
me."

Jesus Christ, the Son of God, is born.

The voice of joy hath sounded in our land ;
the voice of exultation and salvation in the taber-
nacles of sinners. There hath been heard a good
word, a word of consolation, a discourse full of
gladness, worthy of all acceptation. Burst forth
into praises, ye mountains, and all ye trees of
the woods, clap your hands, before the face of
the Lord ; for He hath come. Hear, O heavens,
and give ear, O earth ; be amazed and utter
praises, all creation, but above all, thou, O man.
"Jesus Christ, the Son of God, is born in Beth-
lehem of Judah." Who is there so stony-hearted,
whose soul doth not melt at this word? What
tidings could be sweeter? What proclamation
more delightful? What like unto it hath ever
been heard, or what like unto it hath the world
ever received? O brief word of the abbreviated
Word, but full of celestial sweetness! With
fervent desire I toil, striving to pour forth more
fully full flow of thy honeyed sweetness, but not
finding words.

O birth of spotless sanctity, honourable to
the world, to be loved by men for the greatness
of the benefits conferred on them, and inscrutable
even by angels from the profoundness of its
sacred mystery. The Son of the Highest is born.
God begotten from God before the ages past.
The Word is born a Child. Who indeed can
be sufficiently amazed?

Seek ye the Lord, dearly beloved, while He
may be found ; call ye upon Him while He is
near. Still He must be sought by us with greater
fervour during the Lenten season which is not
only a part of our earthly days, but also a sacrament of them all. If perchance then during
other days our zeal hath somewhat cooled down,
it is fitting that now it should be made to glow
again with spiritual fervour. If the appetite alone
hath sinned, let it alone fast, and it sufficeth.
But if the other members also have sinned, why
should not they fast too? Let the eye accordingly fast, which hath deprived the soul of
treasure ; let the ear fast, let the tongue fast, let
the hand fast, let even the soul itself fast. Let
the eye fast from strange sights and from every
wantonness, so that that which roamed in freedom
in fault-doing may, abundantly humbled, be
checked by penitence. Let the ear, blameably
eager to listen, fast from tales and rumours, and

from whatsoever is of idle import, and tendeth least to salvation. Let the tongue fast from slanders and murmurings, and from useless, vain, and scurrilous words, and sometimes also, in the seriousness of silence, even from things which may seem of essential import. Let the hand abstain from idle signs and from all toils which are not imperatively necessary; but also let the soul herself abstain from all evils and from acting out her own will. For without such abstinence the other things find no favour with the Lord.

Faith and Love.

We have heard from the Apostle that Christ dwelleth in our hearts by faith. Whence it seemeth not unreasonable to understand that Christ liveth in us as long as faith so liveth. But after that our faith is dead, Christ is as it were dead in us. Moreover works are evidence of the life of faith, as it is written: " The works which My Father hath given Me to do, themselves bear witness of Me." And he seemeth not to differ from this utterance, who saith that "faith alone without works is dead." For as we are made aware of the life of the body by its movements, so do we discern the life of faith by its good works. The life of the body is the soul by which it is moved and hath sensation; but the life of faith is charity, because by that it worketh, as thou readest in the Apostle : "Faith which worketh by love." Whence also if love becometh cold, faith dieth, as doth the body when the soul departeth. Thou therefore if thou dost see a man strenuous in good works, and cheerful in the fervour of his intercourse with others, thou dost not doubt that faith liveth in him, having these convincing proofs of his faith being alive.

LXII. SAINT BERNARD ON
LOVING GOD.

On Loving God.

*Loving God is not without its reward, and the
desires of the human heart are not to be
satisfied by earthly things.*

Naturally a man ever desireth something
other than that which he hath. He is contented
with nothing, and whatsoever he hath not he
thinketh better than that which he hath. Whatsoever he hath of beauty, he desireth what is
more beautiful. If he possesseth much wealth,
he envieth one who hath more. Thou mayest see
those who are amply provided with costly things
and valuable property, adding every day field to
field, and with boundless desire extending the
borders of their estates. Thou mayest see also
those who dwell in palatial homes, nevertheless
adding to the same, and with a restless longing
for what is new, ever building, pulling down, and
altering. And as to men raised to high honours,

211   14—2

do we not see them with an insatiable ambition striving with all their strength more and more to attain to higher dignities? And as to all these things there is no final stage, because in them cannot be found aught that is unmistakeably highest or best. What wonder then is it that he who is not content with what is inferior and faulty, is not able to rest satisfied on this side the highest or the best? But this is foolish and of extreme want of insight, to be always desiring those things which never, I do not say satisfy, but even restrain the longings that are felt. Foolish it is, too, inasmuch as whatsoever thou hast of such things thou not the less art eager for what thou hast not, and art ever restlessly panting for the things beyond reach.

*   *   *

> Thou runnest by devious paths, and long before thou reachest by such wanderings the things thou cravest, thou diest.

They who stray around such winding paths, arrive not at any end of blessedness, but are wasted by labour that is in vain. They seek delight in the mere appearances of things rather than in the Creator of them all. They run through the whole range of things, and they desire to make trial of them one by one, without having any care to draw nigh to Him who is the Lord of all. But if indeed they were ever able to have the full mastery of all things, by that law of desire by which they have hungered for what they have not rather than for what they have and have disdained what they have as they have thought of what they have not, they would, having obtained all things in heaven and earth only to despise them, soon at length run to Him, who was alone absent from the things they had longed for—God Himself. Henceforth there would they rest. Just as there is no peace on this side that resolve, so is there no disquietude to disturb them when that resolve hath been reached and passed. This would assuredly be said: "It is good for me to cleave unto God," and "Whom have I in heaven, and apart from Thee whom do I desire upon earth?" and again, "Thou art the God of mine heart, and Thou art my portion for ever." Thus would it be possible for a longing soul to arrive at the highest good, if such soul had before sought eagerly the things not of excellence supreme.

But since that method of attaining such result is altogether impossible, as life is too short and strength insufficient, it is essential that thou must seek God, knowing that He it is who filleth thee with longings for Himself. He Himself prompteth thee to desire. He Himself is what thou desirest.

God Himself is the cause of our loving Him. It
is His love that inspireth our own and rewardeth
it. His love advanceth towards us benignly,
returneth to Him duly, is awaited by us with
gentleness. He is rich towards all who call
upon Him, and yet He hath nothing better than
Himself to give us. Good art Thou, O Lord, to
the soul that seeketh Thee. What art Thou to
the soul that findeth Thee? But in this there is
the marvel, that no one is able to seek Thee
unless he before hath found Thee. Thou desirest
to be found that Thou mayest be sought, and
sought that Thou mayest be found. Thou art
able, in truth, to be sought and to be found, yet
Thou canst not be other than first within us. For
though we say: "In the morning my prayer shall
come before Thee," yet there is not a doubt that
cold would be every prayer which Thine inspiration did not precede.

*   *   *

The first degree of love—the love of self.

It is natural and indeed right that first of all
the Author of Nature should be lovingly served.
Whence the first and greatest command uttered
is: "Thou shalt love the Lord thy God." But
since nature is too fragile and too weak, she is

compelled by an overpowering necessity to prompt
a devotion to self.   Yet lest this love should have
too rapid a flow, or spread itself too widely and
be as a river too little content with its bounding
restraints, flooding too widely the fields around
with the rush of pleasure, then at once its overflow is restrained by the warning command,
"Thou shalt love thy neighbour as thyself."
Most justly indeed should the sharer of our
nature not be as one who hath no share in the
gift of love—that gift which is implanted in our
nature. Whosoever wisheth not to wander beyond
the law of love, let him restrain himself as to his
needs and as to his pleasures, so that he may
minister to the needs and pleasures of others.
Let anyone be indulgent to himself as much as
he desireth, while he at the same time re-
membereth to show the same indulgence to his
neighbour.   But thy love, O man, will be duly
controlled and just, if what thou withdrawest from
thine own pleasures is not withheld from the
needs of a brother. Thus love of self becometh
brotherly love as soon as it seeketh to diffuse
itself over a wider range.

Yet that the neighbour may be loved with
perfect righteousness it is necessary that God
should be in our thoughts. How otherwise is it
possible for one to love his neighbour rightly who

doth not love him in God? Moreover he cannot
love aught in God, who loveth not God Himself.
God therefore must first be loved, that the neighbour may be loved in God. God who is the
Creator of all good things is the Author also of
our love for Himself. He who hath created
Nature also protecteth it. For it was so created
that it might have continually as Protector Him
whom it hath had as Creator. Without Him
nothing could come into existence or be sustained
in existence. Lest the creature should be forgetful of God, and proudly claim, as his own, benefits
that are from the Creator, God, in His deep and
salutary wisdom, hath ordained that man should
be tried by tribulation; so that when man shall
know affliction, and God shall come to his aid,
while man oweth his restoration to God, God by
man, as is fit, may be honoured. For He saith
this : "Call upon Me in the day of tribulation : I
will deliver thee, and thou shalt honour Me."
In this way thus it happeneth, that man, animal
and carnal, who knew not how to love any other
than himself, shall begin to love God even by
reason of himself, and by frequent experience
that in God he is able to do all things—all
things that are good—and that without Him he
can do nothing.

* * *

ON LOVING GOD

The second and third degrees of love.

So then man loveth God, but in the first instance for a while for his own sake, not for the sake of God Himself. There is however a certain prudence in knowing what thou art able to do of thyself, without the aid of God, and to keep thyself from offending Him who keepeth thee unhurt by thyself.

But if frequent tribulation shall assail, on account of which also he again and again turneth to God, and from God repeated deliverance is accorded, would he not, even though his breast were iron and his heart a stone, of a necessity, be softened by the tenderness of his Deliverer until at last he would love God, not on account of his own self alone, but also for God Himself?

As frequent needs render it necessary for man to resort with many entreaties to God, and as by so resorting he experienceth and by experiencing proveth how sweet the Lord is, so it happeneth that the sweetness we experience, more than our own need, urgeth us to love God aright....We speaking to our natural self at length do say: "Now not because of thy necessities we love the Lord, but we have ourselves tasted how sweet the Lord is, and so know of ourselves." For the needs of the lower self are a sort of speech, and announce to us the blessings which they have proved to us by the experience afforded to us.

Thus having advanced, it will not be difficult to fulfil the command as to loving the neighbour. One who loveth God truly, loveth whatsoever is His. Who loveth thus, loveth not otherwise than he is loved, himself seeking no more the things which are his own, but the things of Jesus Christ, even as He hath sought our things, or rather ourselves, and not His own. He who confesseth God, not because He is good to him, but because He Himself is good,—he truly loveth God as God, and not because of himself. This is the third degree of love, with which God is loved, for His own sake.

*   *   *

The fourth degree of love, when man loveth himself, only for God.

Happy is he who hath been worthy to rise to the fourth degree of love, and hath advanced so far as to love himself only for God's sake. When shall my soul, enthralled with divine love, forgetful of herself, having made of herself only a vessel of little worth, be filled with this longing for God, advance towards Him, and lose herself wholly in Him? When shall she say, "My flesh and my heart have fainted away: Thou art the God of mine heart, and the God that is my portion for ever"? I would call him happy and holy to whom it hath been given, rarely it may be, or but once suddenly, for scarcely one moment, to experience something such as this in mortal life. For to love thyself as it were as though thou art not, and altogether to lose consciousness of thyself and to be emptied of thyself, and become almost as naught, this is celestial converse; it is not mere human experience.

Since the Scripture saith that God hath made all things so that His own impress may be on them, assuredly the creature should not fail to conform itself to and to be in accord with the Creator. Accordingly it is for us to turn our desires towards Him, fashioning ourselves not according to our own pleasure but in harmony with His will. Thus it is that we have daily to pray, "Thy will be done on earth, as it is in heaven." O love holy and pure! O tender and sweet affection! O pure and stainless effort of the will! assuredly more stainless and pure in that naught is left in it mingled with the thought of self; tenderer and sweeter inasmuch as the soul is thrilled with a feeling divine. To be thus affected is to be made divine. As a small drop of water, poured into wine, seemeth to lose its own self entirely, while it taketh upon itself both the taste and colour of the wine; and as iron made hot and glowing, becometh very like fire itself, and seemeth to have put off its own pristine and proper form ; and as the air suffused with the light of the sun is transformed into light with all its brilliancy, and seemeth to be not so much illuminated as illumination itself ; so is it that with saintly souls every human affection in a certain ineffable manner, melteth away and is transfused entirely into the will of God. If in man aught of the human were to remain, how should God be all in all ? The substance of human nature will indeed remain, but it will be in another form, with another glory, with another power. When shall this be ? Who will see this? Who will attain to this ? When shall I come and appear in the presence of God? O Lord, my God, mine heart hath said to Thee, " My face hath sought Thee : Thy face, O Lord, will I seek. Deemest Thou me worthy, so that I shall see Thy holy temple ?"

The soul however can only hope to attain to the fourth degree of love, or rather to be caught up to it, when in the spiritual body, the body immortal, pure, calm, and loving, and in all things subject to the spirit. Then, I say, the soul will attain easily to the highest love, when no allurement and no burden of the flesh will hinder her as she hasteneth gladly and eagerly towards the joy of her Lord.

LXIII. SAINT BERNARD ON CONSIDERATION.

[1149—1152 ...... 58—61.]

Addressed to Eugenius III., Bernard of Pisa, Pope from A.D. 1145 to A.D. 1153, and previously a disciple of St Bernard at Clairvaux.

Consideration is not Contemplation.

I do not wish consideration to be understood as being the same in all respects as contemplation. Contemplation concerneth itself with the certainty of things ; consideration more with enquiry into them. So that contemplation may be defined as a true and sure discernment by the mind, or as a laying hold of the truth not at all doubtfully. But consideration is intense mental devotion to enquiry, or the mind's steadfast quest of truth.

*　　*　　*

Four kinds of Consideration.

There are four things that consideration should be devoted to by thee :—thyself, the things below thee, the things around thee, the things above thee.

Let thy consideration begin with thyself, since if thou neglectest thyself, thou wilt in vain extend consideration to other things. What doth it profit thee if thou gainest the whole world, and losest the one important thing, thyself? Although thou mayest be called wise, thou wilt in truth be wanting in wisdom, if thou art not wise as to thyself. Though thou knowest all mysteries, though thou knowest the breadth of the earth, the height of the sky, the depth of the sea, if thou knowest not thyself, thou wilt be like unto one who buildeth without a foundation, making a ruin, not a structure. Whatsoever thou shalt build outside thyself, will be like a heap of dust, at the mercy of the wind. He therefore is not wise, who is not wise towards himself. The wise man will be wise towards himself, and will himself first drink of his own well-spring. So then let thy consideration begin with thyself; but not only that, let it end in thyself. Wheresoever it may wander, call it back to thyself, so that it may bring to thee the fruit of salvation. To thyself be first, to thyself be last. Take example from the Great Father of all, who both sendeth forth His Word and retaineth that Word. Thy word is thy consideration, which if it proceedeth from thee, let it not recede. Let it so go forward that it shall not depart from thee ; let it so go forth that it shall not desert thee. In the quest of salvation let no one be more akin to thee than the only one of thy mother. Think of nothing that is adverse to thine own salvation. "Adverse!"—I have said too little; I ought to have said—"besides." Whatsoever offereth itself to thy consideration, which doth not in any way pertain to thy salvation, cast away.

*   *   *

In this consideration of thyself walk cautiously, and comport thyself with full equity, so that thou mayest neither attribute to thyself more than with truth thou oughtest, nor stint thyself more than would be just. Thou attributest to thyself more than thou truly shouldest, not only by arrogating to thyself goodness which thou hast not, but also by ascribing to thyself goodness which thou hast. Watchfully discern what thou art of thyself, and what thou art by the gift of God, and let there not be any guile in thy mind. But such there will be with thee unless, faithfully separating between what is thine own and what is God's, thou dost assign to Him without insincerity what is His. I do not dispute this that thou art persuaded that the evil in thee is from thyself, the good from the Lord. Whilst considering what kind of man thou art, there must also be re-

223

called to memory what kind of man thou once wast. The later qualities must be compared with the former. Whether hast thou advanced in virtue, in wisdom, in intelligence, in sweetness of manner; or—may it not be so!—hast thou perchance as to these fallen away? Art thou more patient or more impatient than was thy wont, more wrathful or more gentle, more insolent or more humble, more affable or more severe, more yielding to appeals or more unyielding, with more of littlemindedness or more magnanimous, more serious or a little more heedless, more reverential or perchance more recklessly bold than thou oughtest to be? How wide a field stretcheth before thee in this kind of consideration!

Thy zeal should be noted, thy clemency, and thy discretion too, the moderator of those same virtues. With the eye of discretion darkened, either of these virtues is likely to become perverted. There are two causes of this cloudiness of discretion—anger and a too tender sympathy. The latter enfeebleth the censure of a judgment; the former hurrieth it on. The eye disturbed by anger seeth nothing with clemency; the eye suffused with tears flowing with womanly tenderness seeth not aright. Thou wilt not be free from blame, if either thou dost punish him who

ought to be dealt with mercifully, or if thou
sparest him who should be punished.

*   *   *

In tribulations also whatsoever thou hast found
thyself to be, do not thou hide from thyself. If
amid thine own thou hast been unwavering, if as
to those of others thou hast been consolatory,
rejoice. Thus thine heart is aright. But if perchance thou quite otherwise art found to be
restless in thine own, and yet to be scarcely
compassionate towards others in their troubles,
thine heart is most perverse.

What as to thy prosperity? Is there nothing
here that claimeth consideration? Assuredly, if
thou dost take note attentively how rarely one is
to be seen who doth not, though it may be only
slightly, in prosperity set himself loose from self-
watchfulness and discipline. As to discipline,
when hath not prosperity to the heedless been
as fire to wax, as the sun to snow or ice?

Great is he who falling into adversity doth not
fall away even a little from wisdom; and he is
not less great on whom prosperity once present
hath smiled, yet not laughed at. Although thou
wilt more easily find those who have retained
wisdom, when fortune was contrary, than those
who when fortune was propitious have not lost it.

*   *   *

Although the wise man (Ecclus. xxxviii. 25) counselleth that wisdom hath to be written down in the midst of leisure, still leisure, when we have it, must be guarded against. Hence shunned must be idleness, the mother of trifles, the step-mother of virtues. In the worldly trifles are trifles ; in the mouth of the priest they are blasphemies. Yet if sometimes they present themselves, they must perchance be borne with, but never prolonged in talk. Cautiously and prudently ought trifling to be cut short. Some serious thought should be suddenly caught at, which would be hearkened to gladly, and not by reason only of its usefulness, and this would sup-plant the idle words. Thou hast consecrated thy mouth to the Gospel. To open it to speak idle words is forbidden. To constantly utter such is sacrilege. "The lips of the priest keep know-ledge, and law is looked for from his mouth"; certainly not trifles or nonsense. The scurrilous word which is coloured with the name of wit and smartness should be a stranger to thy mouth. That is not enough. It should be cast away far from thine ear.

*   *   *

Thou art before all others, and uniquely so. For what purpose? There is need, I tell thee, of consideration. Is it that thou mayest become of importance through those under you? By no means, but that they may gain importance from thee. They have appointed thee their prince, but for their own good, not for thine. Otherwise how wouldest thou deem thyself superior to those from whom thou cravest benefits? Hear our Lord, "They who have authority over them are called benefactors." But this is concerning them who are without. How doth it apply to us? Thou art called a benefactor falsely if thou intendest not so much to be a benefactor as to be preeminent over benefactors. It is a poor and castdown mind that seeketh not the good of those who are subject to him, but gain that is all for himself. Nothing is more shameful than this in the one who is at the head of all. The Master of the Gentiles saith—that voice of his, ever the same, hath a glory not slight—"I seek not a gift, but fruit."

*   *   *

Let us come to thine associates and fellowhelpers. These are active for thee; these are thine intimates. Wherefore if they are good, to thyself they are most useful. If they are bad they are equally mischievous, more to thyself than to anyone. Thou dost not speak of thyself as well in health, if thou art hurt in thy side; that is to say, thou dost not call thyself good, if thou art trusting to the services of bad men.

If thou art good, what advantage doth thy goodness—the goodness of one man—bring to the Churches of God, when the influence of men otherwise affected hath sway? But thy goodness, if thou art hemmed in by bad men, is not more safe than would be thy bodily health with a serpent close by.

And on the contrary, with good intimates, the more abundant is the help they afford, the oftener it is rendered. But whether thine associates are ot assistance or are a burden, to whom can responsibility be more rightly imputed than to thyself, who hast either chosen or received such into thine intimacy? I speak not of all; for some there are whom thou hast not chosen; but they have attached themselves to thee. Yet no power have they, except what thou hast either granted to them or permitted to them. Leaving out these, the rest, as thou seest, are to be selected or gathered together for the work of this ministry, not without consideration.

It is thy duty to call to thyself and to associate with thyself, whencesoever it may be fitting, after the example of Moses, old men, not young men, but those who are old not so much in age as in character.

And are not they to be chosen from the whole world, who are to judge the world? Let not any

one intrude himself into this work who asketh for
office.   Everything must be arranged by counsel ;
not by yielding to interest.   In the matters which
are strictly our own, there are things which necessarily a petitioner's importunity wresteth from us,
or his necessity deserveth.   But in matters as to
which it is not permitted to me to do as I myself
desire, what foothold hath the petitioner ?   Unless
perchance he who asketh from me aught, asketh
this, that what he wisheth it may be right for me
to wish, and not rather that I may wish it.   One
man asketh for another ; another perchance even
asketh for himself.   The one for whom thou mayest be asked, may be suspected by thee.   He
who himself asketh for himself hath already been
judged.   It is indifferent, whether one asketh
himself, or asketh through another.   A cleric
who frequenteth the court, and who is not of
the court, thou mayest know as belonging to the
set that is always soliciting patronage.   One who
fawneth, or who speaketh what is pleasing to
everybody, deem to be one of the tribe of
petitioners, even though he hath asked for
nothing.   In a scorpion there is nothing about
the face that thou shouldest have fear of ; but
it stingeth by its tail.

If thou shouldest feel thine heart soften, as is
likely, at the blandishments of such, remember

what hath been written: "Every man setteth forth the good wine first, but when they shall have drunk abundantly, then that which is worse." It is the wont of the crafty and deceitful man to make a pretence of humility, when he wisheth to obtain aught. Of such the Scripture saith: "There is that humbleth himself sadly, and yet inwardly is full of deceit." How many whom thou hast admitted as suppliants and afterwards hast had to bear with as moody, insolent, contumacious, rebellious! The perverseness that at first is concealed afterwards cometh forth. The youth of overflowing words, striving after eloquence, while he is empty of wisdom, thou shouldest deem to be not other than a foe to uprightness. As to the false brethren of this sort, the Master saith to thee: "Lay hands suddenly on no man."

Accordingly having kept away the whole of this pestilent race of men, let it be thy care to admit such as afterwards thou wilt not grieve at having admitted. It is disgraceful for thee to have to undo too often what thou hast done, and it is not fitting that thy judgment should be frequently imperilled. Therefore, diligently take counsel with thyself and with those who love thee, as to whatsoever is to be done. Take counsel before aught be attempted, because after, when the thing is done, a retracing of steps is too late. The counsel of the Wise Man is: "Do all things with counsel, and after thou wilt not repent" (Ecclus. xxxii. 19). And persuade thyself of this that it is difficult to be able to test in the court those who are admitted, and, therefore, if it is possible to be done, men who have been tested should be chosen, not those who have to be tested. We in monasteries receive all in the hope of making them better; but the court hath been accustomed to welcome men who are good, rather than to make them good. But if however we have shown there have been at the court more good men who have fallen short of the excellences required than there have been faulty men who have improved, then certainly they ought to be sought for, in whom failure need not be feared, nor improvement desired, inasmuch as they already have attained to the fitting perfection.

Select therefore not the willing, and not the eager, but the hesitating, the reluctant; even urge these, compel these, to come in. Thy spirit may find rest, as I think, in such as are not of shameless brow, but are modest and reverent, who fear no one, but God only, who hope for nothing except from God; who observe not the hands of those who draw near to them, but their necessities; who stand up manfully for the afflicted, and give

judgment in equity for the meek upon earth, who
are of well-ordered manners, tested as to their
holiness, prepared for obedience, meek in suffering, submissive to discipline, severe in cen-
suring, Catholic as to faith, faithful in steward-
ship; who are of one mind with each other in
desires for peace, who alike with one another
work for unity; who are righteous in judgment,
prudent in counsel, discreet in authority, in-
dustrious in setting things in order, strenuous
in action, modest in speech, in adversity undisturbed, in prosperity devout, in zeal restrained, in
kind actions not remiss, in leisure not idle, in
hospitality not too lavish, as to banquets not
overmuch given to them, in care of private
affairs not anxious, of others' goods not covetous,
of their own not wasteful, everywhere and in all
things circumspect; who when an embassy hath
to be assigned for Christ, would neither if ordered
to take it up, decline it, nor when not invited
would be eager for the task; who what they
would modestly excuse themselves from, would
not too obstinately refuse; who when sent, would
not go after gold, but would follow Christ; who
would esteem their mission not as undertaken for
gain, and would look not for recompense but for
fruitful results; who would not despise the common
people, but teach them; who the rich do not flatter

but speak rousingly to, the poor do not burden,
but cherish; who the threats of princes do not
fear, but despise; who do not begin their work
with noisy display, or bring it to a close with
anger; who do not despoil churches, but restore
them; who do not empty purses, but touch hearts,
and correct wrong-doing; who are heedful of their
own repute, and do not envy another his; who
have a steadfast zeal in prayer, and are so disposed to prayer as to trust more to it than to their
own industry and toil; whose coming is peaceful,
whose departure is lamented; whose speech is
edification, whose life is justice itself, whose
presence is gratifying, whose memory is blessed;
who show themselves to be lovable not in word
simply but in deed also; who show themselves
worthy of reverence, but by their doings not by
proud display; who are humble with the humble,
and with the innocent are innocent; who severely
rebuke the hardened; who keep in check the
malignant; who deal retribution to the proud;
who hasten not to enrich themselves or their
families with the dowry of the widow or with
the patrimony of the Crucified; who freely give
what they have freely received; who give without
price judgment in favour of those who suffer from
injustice; who give freedom to nations, rebukings
to peoples; who, like unto the seventy chosen by

Moses, are seen to have received of thine own spirit, by which whether absent or present, they earnestly endeavour in thine absence to please thee and to please God ; who return to thee, wearied indeed, but not surfeited with gifts, at the same time boasting not because they have brought to thee curious and precious things of the lands from which they have returned, but because they have left behind them peace to kingdoms, law for barbarians, quiet for monasteries, order for the churches, discipline for the clergy, a people acceptable unto God, striving to attain unto good works.

*   *   *

I think it appropriate to tell of an incident relating to our own Martin, of sweet memory. Thou hast heard it ; but whether thou rememberest it, I do not know. He, a cardinal presbyter, had for some time acted as legate in Dacia. He returned so poor, that with money almost gone and horses become unfit for use, he got with difficulty to Florence. There the bishop of the place gave him a horse, on which he rode to Pisa, where we then were. On the next day—so I think it was— there came following him the bishop, who had a law-suit with an opponent, with the day of hearing drawing nigh, and who began to ask for the votes of his friends. When he had solicited them one

by one, he came to Martin. Then said Martin:
"Thou hast deceived me; I did not know that
this matter was on hand. Take thine horse;
yonder it is in the stable." And the same hour
he gave it back to him. What sayest thou to
that, my Eugenius? Is it not an affair of another
age?—this coming back of a legate, from a land
of gold, without gold? this traversing a land of
silver, and knowing nothing of silver? and, as
well, this rejecting on the spot a gift which might
be suspected?

But O! I am delighted that an opportunity
presenteth itself of recalling to memory and men-
tioning a name of sweetest fragrance, that of
Bishop Gaufridus of Carnotes, who at his own
charges strenuously carried on an embassy in
Aquitaine, and that for many years. I speak of
what I saw myself. I was with him in that
country when by a certain priest there was presented to him a fish which is commonly called a
sturgeon. The legate asked how much it would
cost. "I do not accept it," he said, "unless thou
receivest its price." And he handed over five
golden shillings to the unwilling and ashamed
priest.

Again, when we were in a certain town, a lady
of that town, out of devotedness, offered to him,
with a towel, two or three side dishes, beautifully

wrought, but of wood. The man of scrupulous conscience, when he had looked at them for some time, spoke in praise of them, but would not consent to receive them. Would he who had refused wooden plates, have accepted silver ones?

O if there could be given to us a supply of men such as these we have now alluded to, who would be happier than thou? What age could be more delightful? Would not the blessedness of those times seem to thee second only to that of eternity, when in whatsoever direction thou didst move, thou wouldest see thyself surrounded with so splendid an array of blessed ones?

If I know thee, thou art embarrassed. Drawing a deep sigh thou speakest to thyself: "Thinkest thou that what thou hast spoken of is possible to happen? When shall these things be? Who may live to see them? O if I might see in my lifetime the Church of God sustained by such columns! O if I might behold the Spouse of my Lord committed to such great faithfulness, entrusted to such great purity! How I should be more than blest, if I could see around me men of this kind as the guardians and also as the witnesses of my life! To such all my secrets I might safely commit, my counsels I might communicate; to such I might unbosom myself entirely as to another self. Such, if I were to wish to wander in some sort of way out of the right path, would not permit me; they would restrain me from precipitousness; they would arouse me out of any slumbering; of such the reverence and due freedom would repress me if I should be overbearing, would set me right if I should step beyond my duty; of such the constancy and fortitude would strengthen me if I should be frail, would set me upright if I should falter; of such the faith and sanctity would provoke me to undertake whatsoever things are holy, whatsoever things are honourable, whatsoever things are modest, whatsoever things are lovable and of good report."

And now, my Eugenius, turn thine eyes upon that which is the present state of the court and of the Church, and upon the aims of the prelates, especially of those who are within the circle of which thou art at the very centre.

* * *

Of the court, enough; the palace let us quit; at home they await us.

This is not an over-abundant consideration, this one as to how thou intendest to order thine household, to provide for those who are in thy lap and in thy bosom. This is, I say, also, a necessary consideration. Listen to Paul: "If a man knoweth not how to rule his own house, how shall he take care of the Church of God ? " And as I say these things I do not counsel thee, devoted as thou art to highest things, to become taken up with the lowest, to become as it were lost in details, and to spend on paltry things what thou owest to the greatest things. Still such little things have to be done, while the great things have not to be omitted. While the great things are done by thyself, thou must also provide such as for thee will attend to the small things. For if one servant alone sufficeth not for taking care of the cattle and attending to the tables, how canst thou by thyself alone attend both to thine own house and to the house of the Lord at the same time? Thy mind ought to be set free from care for things of a low and mean order, because it hath to be intent on matters very great and very varied.

Someone must be procured to entangle himself, as it were, in the rough work of grinding for thee. For thee, I say, not with thee. Some things thou wilt do thyself; some things thyself and others together with thee will do; other things others without thee will attend to.

Surely not as to such things as these will thy consideration sleep. I indeed think that the details of thine household must be placed under the heading that I have mentioned last. Thou wilt attend to them by another. But he, if he is not faithful, will defraud ; if he is not prudent, will be defrauded. Hence there must be sought for one both faithful and prudent, whom thou mayest place over thine household. Yet he is useless if a third essential is wanting. Dost thou ask what this is? Authority. Therefore there must be given to him the power of acting as seemeth best to him. If thou thinkest this not accordant with reason, remember that he is faithful, and desireth to act with reason, and forget not that he is prudent and knoweth how to act with reason. But a faithful and alert will can act to advantage only when it is subsequently upheld, so that there is made over to it a complete facility for the performance of duty, with unhesitating obedience from all. Therefore all must be submissive to him. Let him have to endure no contradictory temper. Let there be no one who may say, "Why hast thou done this?" Let him have the power to dismiss and engage and to change servants, and to transfer duties as and when he wisheth. Let him be so feared by all that he may benefit all. Let him be at the head of all so that he may be in all things advantageous to them all. Secret and whispered complaints against him, do not give heed to : censure rather the faultfinders.

Thus let one appoint to all the others their

work, and let them all be answerable to the one.
Do thou have faith in that one, and so keep thyself free for thyself and the Church of God. If
one is found who would be faithful, and another
who would be prudent, the service to be administered should be entrusted to the one likely to be
faithful. Assuredly this is the safer of the two
selections before thee. Still if a fit person is not
found, I counsel thee rather to select one likely
to fail in fidelity, rather than to plunge thyself
into what will be a labyrinth. Remember that
our Saviour had for His steward a Judas. What
is more disgraceful for a bishop than to be
cumbered with cares as to furniture and as to
scraps of property? to be scrutinising everything,
to be questioning about everything, to be eaten
up with suspicions, to be troubled about everything lost or neglected? I mention this to the
shame of some who are every day reckoning up
all their possessions, counting every single one,
exacting a statement as to pence and farthings.
Not thus untrustful was that Egyptian who entrusted all to Joseph, and knew not what he had
in his house. A Christian should blush who
trusteth not a Christian with his goods. A man
without faith had faith in his servant, and placed
him over all his goods, and this servant was one
from a strange land.

Wonderful! Bishops have at hand enough and more than enough men to whom they entrust the care of souls, and find not one to whom to confide their small possessions! Forsooth they must be the very best in knowing the value of things who take great care of the least, and little or none of the greatest! As to the price of food and the number of loaves there is daily discussion with servants; rarely now is there a conference with priests on the sins of the people! An ass falleth, and there is someone to lift it up; a soul is perishing, and there is no one to care for it! No wonder, when we are not conscious of our own habitual failings! At every one of these calculations of ours, are we not angry, do we not get hot, are we not worried? How much more patiently should we put up with the loss of our earthly things than with the loss of human souls! "Why," saith one, "do ye not rather suffer yourselves to be defrauded?" Thou who teachest others, teach thyself. I pray thee, if already thou hast not done so, to hold thyself as of more value than the things that are thine own. Those transitory things that in no way are able to stay with thee, cause them to pass by thee, not through thee. A river wherever it ploweth, scoopeth out the earth; so the passage of temporal things through the thoughts eateth away the conscience. If a flood can rush over the fields without hurt to the growing corn, thou also mayest trust to be able to drag such things as these through thy mind without a wound to it. I counsel thee to study to avert from thee, howsoever thou canst, the rush of such things as these. Of many thou shouldest be ignorant, of very many thou shouldest seem to be unconscious, of some thou shouldest be forgetful.

But I wish thee not to be ignorant of the manners and pursuits of thine attendants. It is not fitting that thou shouldest be the last to know of the faults of thine household. Wherefore, as I have said, let another control everything else; but as to the discipline, do thou look after that; entrust that to no one. If before thine eyes speech should sound insolently, or apparel should seem unbecoming, let thine hand be upon such things; do thou punish what is an offence against thyself. Impunity produceth boldness, boldness excess. Sanctity becometh the home of a bishop; modesty becometh it; praiseworthiness becometh it. Of these, discipline is the guardian. The priests of the household are either honoured by others, or give rise to talk in all. In the looks, in the attire, in the demeanour of those who are around thee, do thou suffer nothing immodest, nothing unbecoming.

Yet it is not austerity that I counsel, but gravity. Austerity driveth away the weak ones; gravity represseth the too frivolous. Austerity, if it is present, rendereth one hateful; gravity, if it is absent, causeth one to be despised. Still in all things moderation is to be preferred. I would not have thee too severe, or too easy-going. What is more pleasing than that moderation possessing which thou art neither burdensome from severity nor contemptible from familiarity? In the palace show thyself to be Pope, at home the father. Let thine attendants love thee; if they do not, take care that they fear thee. The guarding of the lips is always useful, and yet such should not drive out the grace of affability. Therefore everywhere the too-ready tongue should be restrained, but especially at the feast. That bearing will be the most suitable, with which thou wilt be in action grave, in look benignant, in speech earnest.

*   *   *

Consider before all things the Holy Roman Church, over which by the authority of God thou presidest, to be the mother of the Churches, not the mistress. Look upon thyself not as the lord of the bishops but as one of them; moreover think of thyself as the brother of those who love God and as a partaker with them that fear

Him. Consider also that thou oughtest to be a model of uprightness, a mirror of holiness, an example of piety, the assertor of truth, the defender of the faith, the teacher of nations, the leader of Christians, the friend of the Bridegroom, the leader to her Spouse of the Bride, the ordainer of the clergy, the shepherd of the people, the instructor of the foolish, the refuge of the oppressed, the advocate of the poor, the hope of the wretched, the guardian of the fatherless, the renderer of justice to widows, the eye of the blind, the tongue of the dumb, the staff of the old, the avenger of crimes, the fear of the malignant, the glory of the good, a rod for the powerful, a hammer for tyrants, the father of kings, the moderator of laws, the dispenser from canons, the salt of the earth, the light of the world, the priest of the Most High, the vicar of Christ, the anointed of the Lord. Understand what I say; the Lord will give thee understanding. When power is joined to wickedness, thou must be presumed to be something more than man. Thy face must be upon them that do evil. Let him who feareth not man, who dreadeth not the sword, fear the breath of thy wrath. Let him who hath despised thine admonition fear thy prayer. Let him with whom thou art angry think that with him, not man, but God, is angry. Who hath not heard thee, let him

tremble at the thought that God will hear thee
and will be against him.

*   *   *

Hitherto, consideration hath been dealt with
in relation to action, inasmuch as it hath been
taught or admonished that some things should
not only be considered, but also done. But the
things which are above, which have now to be
dealt with, are not in want of action, but require
contemplation. Advance is now made to the
realm of spirit. That realm is our God, the
Almighty Spirit, the great mansion of the spirits
of the blessed. That realm is truth; it is wisdom,
virtue, eternity, the highest good.

*   *   *

The greatest of all men is he, who discarding
the use of visible things and of the senses, as far
as is permitted to human frailty, hath accustomed
himself, not by ascending steps, but by transcendent
departures, to fly upwards in contemplation to the
sublimest heights. The raptures of Paul, I deem,
were of this kind. An instantaneous translation,
not a gradual ascent, was what he experienced,
for he himself setteth forth not that he ascended,
but that he was rather caught up into Paradise.

*   *   *

Three kinds of consideration may be noted.
The consideration which useth the senses and

245

sensible things in our dealings with one another, so as to become acceptable unto God. The consideration which thoughtfully and diligently enquireth into everything and pondereth over everything in order to find God. The consideration which collecteth all one's thoughts inwardly, and, as far as one is divinely aided, severeth from human concerns in order to contemplate God.

*   *   *

Dost thou think that I can speak what the eye hath not seen, nor the ear hath heard, and what hath not welled up in the heart of man? "To us," the apostle saith, " God hath revealed them by His Spirit." The things above then are not taught by speech, but are revealed by the Spirit. But what speech doth not unfold, let consideration seek, prayer aspire to, the life be worthy of, purity reach unto.

Yet when thou art admonished as to the things that are above, think not that thou art sent by me to behold the sun, the moon, the stars, no, not the sky itself, not the waters which are above the sky. All these things though in position above are in true value, and in dignity of nature, beneath thee, for they are material. That which is spiritual is thine, and thus in vain dost thou look above for anything which is not spirit. Moreover God is

ON CONSIDERATION

Spirit and the holy angels are so too, and these
are above thee. God and the blessed spirits who
are with Him, are by three methods, or by as many
paths, by our consideration to be sought for—by
opinion, faith, and understanding. Of these, understanding relieth on reason, faith on authority, while
opinion justifieth itself only by its likeness to truth.
The first two have certain truth ; but faith discerneth truth, hidden and obscure though it be ;
understanding possesseth it naked and manifest ;
but opinion having nothing sure seeketh truth by
resemblances rather than graspeth it.

*   *   *

As to God, this He Himself wished to be given
as an answer, this He taught and Moses spake
unto the people, He Himself enjoining him: "He
who is hath sent me to you." Nothing could more
fittingly tell of eternity, God being eternal. If
thou shouldest say of God that He is good, great,
blessed, wise, or is any other such excellence, it
hath its origin in this word, that He is, God is.

Again do we ask, What is God? That without
which nothing is. Nothing can exist without Him,
just as He Himself cannot exist without Himself.
He is the beginning of all things.

What is God? He for whom the centuries
have neither come nor departed, nor are co-
eternal with him. What is God? He from

whom are all things, through whom are all things, in whom are all things. Thou askest, "If all things are in God, where is He Himself?" I cannot find one place where alone He is. What place could contain Him? Thou askest, "Where is He not?" And this I indeed cannot tell. What place is without God? God is not present in any limited space. He is present everywhere. He who is not enclosed by space is nowhere; and He who is not excluded by any space must be everywhere. In His own sublime and transcendent way, as all things are in Him, so is He in all things. Where He was before the world was, there He is. Thou must not. ask, "Where was He?" Besides Himself there was nothing. Therefore He was in Himself.

*　　*　　*

Perchance it will not be to thy taste if I again ask, What is God? both because the question hath been so often asked, and because thou art distrustful as to an answer being found. I tell thee, Eugenius, my father, God is He alone who can never be sought in vain, even when He cannot be found. As to this, thine own experience may teach thee; or, if not, believe one who hath had experience, not myself, but a holy one who saith, "Thou art good, O Lord, to them that hope in Thee, to the soul that seeketh Thee." What

then is God? Of the universe He is the final
end; as to election, He is salvation; as to
Himself, He hath knowledge. What is God?
Omnipotent will, virtue of highest benevolence,
light eternal, reason unchangeable, highest blessedness; Creator of minds to receive of His own
fulness, imparting to them life to be conscious of
Him, prompting them to desire Him, enlarging
them to receive Him, fitting them to be worthy of
Him, enkindling them with zeal, aiding them to
yield fruit, directing them to equity, fashioning
them to benevolence, tempering them for wisdom,
strengthening them for virtue, visiting them for
consolation, illuminating them for knowledge,
preserving them for immortality, enriching them
for felicity, surrounding them with protection.

*   *   *

What is God? The punishment of the perverse not less than the glory of the humble. For
He is a reasonable, unchangeable, and unswerving
equity, having touch with all everywhere.

*   *   *

What is God? Length, breadth, height and
depth.

Length, I say. What is that? Eternity.
This is so long that it hath no end, not more
in place than in time.

He is also breadth. And what is that? Love.

With what bounds is love hemmed in in God, who hateth nothing that He hath made? For He maketh the sun to shine upon the good and the evil, and sendeth rain over the just and the unjust. Therefore His bosom embraceth also His enemies. And not even content with this, Divine Love spreadeth out into infinity. It exceedeth not only affection, but knowledge also, for the Apostle aspireth "to know the love of Christ which transcendeth knowledge."

What again is God? Height and depth. In the one He is above all things; in the other He is below all things. Consider His power—its height, His wisdom—its depth. His height—His sublimity—is far beyond reach. His depth—His profoundness—is inscrutable. Paul, in accents of wonder, saith: "O the depth of the riches of the wisdom and knowledge of God! how unsearchable are His judgments, and His ways how past finding out!" We, too, contemplating power and wisdom in God, and their perfect unity with God, may exclaim: "O powerful wisdom, reaching everywhere mightily! O wise power, planning all things sweetly!"

LXIV. SAINT BERNARD'S HYMN
IN PRAISE OF JESUS.

I. *Jesu dulcis memoria.*

Jesus, our thoughts of Thee are sweet;
They make our hearts with joy to beat;
But sweeter 'tis that evermore
Thy presence here we may adore.

No softer music doth entrance,
No words so our delight enhance,
No sweeter thought hath love so won
Than that of Jesus, God's dear Son.

O hope of those who pardon need,
How merciful to those who plead!
To those who seek Thee Thou art kind,
But, what art Thou to those who find?

No tongue is able to express,
No words can tell, the blissfulness
He only who hath tried can know
What joys, from loving Jesus flow.

Be Thou, O Jesus, our great bliss;
Be Thou the prize we shall not miss;
In Thee may we Thy glory share
In endless joy beyond compare.

251

SAINT BERNARD'S HYMN

II. *Jesu, Rex admirabilis.*

O Jesus, Thee we praise as King!
Thee, Winner of our souls, we sing!
The sweetness words cannot express
Of Thine unblemished loveliness.

When Thou dost come within the heart,
Thy truth doth then clear light impart;
The world's vain things lose their appeal,
Thy love's pure glow within we feel.

Thou to our hearts dost sweetness bring,
For world of souls the living Spring!
Thou for our minds the Heavenly Light,
Our joys and hopes surpassing quite!

O trust in Jesus, every one;
Pray that His love be missed by none.
For Jesus seek with ardent zeal;
His love's pure flame will round thee steal.

Jesus, may each voice sound Thy name!
Thy deeds, by us wrought, spread Thy fame!
May our hearts' love entwine round Thee,
Both now and for eternity!

IN PRAISE OF JESUS

III. *Jesu, decus angelicum.*

O Jesus, joy of angel throng,
In every ear the sweetest song,

In every mouth honey divine,
In every heart celestial wine!

They who Thee taste crave as at first;
They who Thee drink are still athirst.

With naught but earnest gaze above,
They yearn for Jesus whom they love.

Jesus, to me most dear Thou art,
The hope of mine aspiring heart;

With tears of love for Thee I sigh;
For Thee mine inmost soul doth cry.

Abide with us in this our night,
And shed on us, O Lord, Thy light;

From out our souls dispel all gloom,
And make the world with sweetness bloom.

O Jesus, Maiden Mother's Flower,
On us may Thy love's sweetness shower.

Thine the praise ! Thy Name's honour Thine !
Thine the kingdom of bliss divine !

SAINT BERNARD'S HYMN

IV. *Amor Jesu dulcissimus.*

The love of Jesus is most sweet
And is with tenderness complete,

Welcome more a thousand-fold
Than can in uttered words be told.

Jesus I'll seek as I rest apart
In close-shut chamber of mine heart.

Alone, or as mid throngs I move
I'll seek Him with untiring love.

With Mary, as the dawn doth loom,
I'll seek my Jesus in the tomb,

And, as my heart doth sigh and cry,
I'll look, with soul's, not body's, eye.

With bitter tears I'll flood the tomb,
Will mourn and cry within its gloom.

Jesus, at Thy feet, I'll sink;
In Thine embrace Thou wilt me link.

His bitter Passion this doth show,
For this His sacred blood doth flow,

That our redemption He might gain
And we to sight of God attain.

254

IN PRAISE OF JESUS

V. *Jesu, auctor clementiæ.*

O Jesus, pity's one true source,
To Thee, joy's hope, all have recourse!

Spring of sweetness! fount too of grace!
The gladness true that hearts embrace!

Then love ye Him who you doth love;
The love ye get return above;

In search of love's sweet odour haste;
Thus His love's path will be retraced.

Good Jesus, so that I may know
In full abundance Thy love's glow,

Thy presence grant I may behold,
Thy glory Thou to me unfold.

E'en when unfit I am aright
To sing of Thee, not silent quite

May I be; but may my voice
With love inspired, in Thee rejoice.

Jesus, Thy love, most welcome dole,
Is food refreshing for the soul,

Is ever grateful, never tires,
Meeteth, not quencheth, all desires.

255

SAINT BERNARD'S HYMN

VI. *Quem tuus amor ebriat.*

In whom Thy love doth overflow,
His is the joy that Thou dost know.

Happy he whom Thy love doth bless;
Naught else he craveth to possess.

A thousand times I long for Thee.
Jesus, when wilt Thou come to me?

When wilt Thyself with me be found?
When wilt Thy joy in me abound?

Thy love unceasingly is bright,
To me an ever-near delight,

To me a fruit like honey sweet,
A fruit for life eternal meet.

Thy love it doth transcend desire;
Naught else than it do I require.

Henceforth for me let all things fade,
So I may live with Thy love's aid.

O wheresoe'er I shall abide,
Jesus I'll wish for at my side.

What joy to meet Him on my way!
What bliss for Him with me to stay!

IN PRAISE OF JESUS

VII. *Jesu, summa benignitas.*

Thy mercy reacheth to the skies;
Thy joy doth bid my wonder rise.

Thy goodness hath a boundless reign;
May Thy love guide me with its chain.

What glad embrace when Thee we meet!
What draughts of honeyed converse sweet,

When rapt in Thee! O happy day!
Too soon, too soon, to pass away!

What I have asked that now I see,
What longed for, that I have in Thee.

In Thy dear love whilst I do thrill,
Mine heart with yearnings warm doth fill.

When Thou lov'st us, and we love Thee,
Such love doth last eternally,

Never faileth, never fadeth,
Ever groweth, ever gloweth.

Burneth always this love of Thine!
How wondrous sweet this love now mine!

Yea, Thine and mine, it hath delights,
Delights that rise to happy heights.

SAINT BERNARD'S HYMN

VIII. *Hic amor missus coelitus.*

This heaven-sent love doth cling and rest
In the recesses of my breast.

My mind it setteth all on fire,
My soul it urgeth to aspire.

O blessed fire of heavenly love!
O yearnings kindled from above!

O the sweet consolation won
In loving Jesus, God's dear Son!

O come, O come, most glorious King,
Whose praises all do long to sing!

More brightly in us do Thou shine
With hoped-for glory wholly Thine.

Thou, than the sun more bright, more calm,
More sweet than the most fragrant balm.

Sweeter far than all sweetness sprung
'Mid pleasures of the worldly throng.

Thou dost so much refresh the soul;
Thy fragrance hath such sweet control.

In Thee I lose this self of mine!
Mine own heart's love is lost in Thine.

IN PRAISE OF JESUS

IX. *Tu mentis delectatio.*

In Thee delighteth full the mind,
And love doth highest being find.

My glory I discern in Thee,
And all do find salvation free.

Thou, my lov'd Lord, hast for Thine own
The glory of the Father's throne,

Hast conquered here by might of love
And now dost reign in Heaven above.

Where Thou shalt go I too must be;
Thou can'st not e'er be far from me,

Since Thou away hast borne mine heart,
Thou in whose praises all take part.

Ye citizens of heaven, draw nigh!
Your gates lift up, lift up on high!

Sing loud to the Triumphant One:
Hail! Jesus, King of glory won!

King of valour, King of glory!
King renowned in victory's story!

Giver of grace with lavish hand,
Thou honour of the heavenly land!

X. *Tu fons misericordiae.*

Fount from which springeth mercy's stream,
Let truth's bright lamp upon us gleam ;

From round us chase sorrow's dark night ;
Guide us upwards with glory's light.

The choirs of heaven to Thee sing praise ;
Their echoed songs they ever raise.

Thou fillest souls with joy on earth ;
Man's peace with God is brought to birth.

Jesus doth reign in perfect peace
That maketh all unrest to cease.

'Tis peace for which my soul hath yearned
So that its joys may soon be earned.

Jesus to the Paternal Throne
Hath gone on high, and there doth own

Mine heart's aspiring, loyal love,
Which ever followeth Him above.

Him we follow with our love's praise,
Vows, hymns, and prayers to Him we raise,

That He will grant to us above
Mansions with Him of joy and love.

Amen.

LXV. SAINT BERNARD'S PRAYER
TO CHRIST UPON THE CROSS.

I. *Salve, mundi salutare.*

Hail! Saviour Christ, who dost set free
The world from sin and misery.
Should I but wish like Thee to die
Nailed to Thy Cross, Thou would'st know why.
      O give to me
      Support from Thee.

When Thou dost here to us draw nigh,
When Thou art with us from on high,
Divinely pure Thou dost appear.
As I in lowliness come near,
      Thy grace bestow
      As I fall low.

The nails, with their so rough impress,
Gently and sadly I caress;
The marks which cruelty did trace
I with affection do embrace.
      Wounds, bruises Thine;
      Remembrance mine.

SAINT BERNARD'S PRAYER

For Thy charity so boundless
We thank Thee, though in sore distress.
Thou pardon dost in love impart,
O Healer of the broken heart!
       Their Father sweet
       Thy poor entreat.

Whatever is in me at fault
In act all wrong, with wrong distraught,
Do Thou, sweet Jesus, Thy power reveal;
Do Thou restore. O do Thou heal
       With soothing wine
       Of love divine.

Thee on Thy Cross, O Lord, I seek,
As I can, with heart pure and meek.
Me Thou wilt heal; my hope is such.
Reach to me with Thy healing touch,
       By life-stream laved,
       By Thy Cross saved.

Thy wounds and scars with crimson tints
And the deeply impressed nail-prints,
Do Thou inscribe upon mine heart,
That so in Thee I may have part,
       And love display
       In every way.

TO CHRIST UPON THE CROSS

O sweet Jesus, in love for all
Yielding Thy life ! to Thee I call ;
Extend to me Thy pardon's sway ;
Though faulty, spurn me not away
      From Thy dear feet
      As one not meet.

Before Thy Cross myself I fling,
To Thy feet I humbly cling.
Good Jesus, do not Thou me spurn,
On Thy sacred Cross toward me turn.
      With love divine
      Thine head incline.

From the Cross, where Thou art raised high
Look on me, loved Lord, as I lie.
Take Thou me captive, win my soul,
Say Thou in mercy : " Be thou whole."
      To Thee I yield
      What Thou hast healed.

II. *Salve, Jesu, rex sanctorum.*

Jesus, King of Saints, all hail !
Sinners' hope that doth not fail.
On Cross of wood, as if crime Thine,
Hanging as man and yet Divine,
       Seeming as soon
       Thou would'st swoon.

O Christ, despised, disrobed, forlorn,
Made on the Cross a mark for scorn,
Gazed on by those who at Thee jeer,
Submitting meekly, without fear.
       In Thy limbs worn
       Of all strength shorn.

Thy life-blood, in abundance shed,
With ceaseless flow, to feet from head.
Completely laved with Thine own blood
As in grief's majestic flood;
       Yet hostile eyes
       Thy garb despise.

O Thine infinite Majesty!
O unheard-of humility!
Who in truth with love like Thine own
Hath sought and left Thee not alone,
       Suffering giving
       For Thy suffering?

TO CHRIST UPON THE CROSS

O what shall I before Thee plead
I hard in heart, worthless in deed?
What to my soul's Lover repay,
Whom for me wicked hands do slay,
       So that not I
       Doubly should die?

This love of Thine, this love so strong,
To realm of death doth not belong;
This my thought will never perish,
How Thou dost me clasp and cherish,
       Lest death its sting
       At me should fling.

When of Thy pure love I think,
From clasping Thee I fain would shrink;
But 'tis with love that I draw nigh;
To Thee I come; Thou knowest why.
       Do Thou sustain;
       Show not disdain.

Not what I do let burden Thee;
But do Thou heal, do Thou cleanse me,
Just as I am, defiled and ill.
May this Thy blood flow o'er me till
       Not one slight stain
       May e'er remain.

SAINT BERNARD'S PRAYER

On this Thy Cross, to Thee blood-stained,
Nailed, tortured, and by all disdained,
That I may pray, do Thou inspire
And this my wish fulfil entire,
      That as I pray
      I act alway.

That I may pray with mind all bent
On Thee, O may my chief intent
Be, not 'scaping toil howe'er mean,
But being healed, by Thee made clean,
      When I find place
      In Thine embrace.

TO CHRIST UPON THE CROSS

III. *Salve, Jesu, pastor bone.*

Hail, dear Jesus, Thou Shepherd Good,
Worn out in strife, misunderstood,
Thy limbs out-stretched on Cross of wood;
On Cross of wood nailed for man's good
      Thy holy hands
      Do bless far lands.

O holy hands, all hail to you;
Ye are filled with roses new,
With roses red from each rough scar
With which the cruel nails do mar,
      From which there flow
      The drops which glow.

Lo! there floweth in showers fine
From each transfixèd hand of Thine
Thy life-blood, in drops abundant,
Red like roses, blooming, fragrant,
      Salvation's cost
      To free the lost.

Those hands by nails so pierced and pained,
And by Thy life-blood purple-stained
The stream that from Thine heart floweth,
To us in need Thy love showeth,
      As drop by drop
      It doth not stop.

267

SAINT BERNARD'S PRAYER

O how gen'rous, Thee Thyself to give
That evil ones and good may live.
Both the heedless and the earnest
In Thine out-stretched arms find true rest.
      Thou with love's call
      Welcomest all.

Lo! I present myself to Thee,
Whom scarred and wounded now I see;
O on sad souls pardon bestow,
To me forbearance ever show,
      For Thou dost shield
      All who love yield.

As at Thy Cross, Lord, I do wait,
All mine affection captivate.
May I Thy Cross so love and know
As 'neath it toil to undergo.
      I come to Thee;
      Embrace Thou me.

On the wide path of love divine,
Guide me into all truth of Thine.
Before this Cross of Thine so dear
Help me to find love's victory near.
      Deeds that offend
      For ever mend.

TO CHRIST UPON THE CROSS

Ye holy hands, you I embrace,
And though I moan, delight to trace
And give thanks for, the wounds ye show,
For nails so hard, for drops that flow,
       And sighing much
       With kisses touch.

In Thy blood I by Thee made pure
Give myself to Thee, and adjure
These sacred hands of Thine, O Lord
Defence and aid to me afford
       In danger's hour
       With Thy love's power.

SAINT BERNARD'S PRAYER

IV. *Salve, Jesu, summe bonus.*

Good Jesus, hail! on souls Thine own
To have mercy so wondrous prone,
Torture keen Thy limbs so slender
Endure for long, though so tender.
   Outstretched on Cross
   Thou suff'rest loss.

Heart of Saviour, which our hearts greet,
In which storeth honey so sweet,
In which showeth Thy love so strong,
From which floweth a stream among
   Our souls to lave
   That sins deprave.

O Jesus! I to Thee draw near;
Do Thou me spare, though I have fear;
To Thee I come with shame-marked brow;
To Thee I come; how freely now,
   A sinful man,
   Thy wounds to scan.

O wound of love, thou aperture,
From which doth flow a stream so pure;
O portal deep that doth still show
More than rose-like crimson glow,
   Displaying power
   To heal this hour.

TO CHRIST UPON THE CROSS

Thy fragrance, all wine excelleth ;
Serpent's venom it repelleth.
Who drink of Thee of life partake.
Come ye who wish your thirst to slake ;
  This wound for you
  Is sweet to view.

O ruddy wound, make thine appeal,
So cause mine heart with thee to feel,
That I in thee myself may hide,
And may in rapture there abide.
  Do thou respond
  To heart so fond.

My lips touch thee with pure salute
I cling with adoration mute :
With thee mine heart mingleth in bliss,
Blendeth as one with sacred kiss.
  So with transport
  I am upcaught.

How truly sweet Thy love to know,
O Jesus Christ, and in Thee grow.
Thus ever with Thy sweetness nigh
For very love I could e'en die.
  Thy love to own
  Is life alone.

SAINT BERNARD'S PRAYER

In this retreat hide me apart,
In rest profound bury mine heart,
There in Thyself with love to glow,
There with Thyself in peace to grow,
      In peace so dear
      With naught to fear.

In my last hour, O may my soul
Find rest in Thee and Thy control,
Be so enwrapt till latest breath
That naught can bring a taint of death.
      O thus to stay
      Through love's long day!

TO CHRIST UPON THE CROSS

Jesus, my Divine Salvation,
Worthy of all adoration !
Should not to Thy most sacred breast
Words of reverence be addressed—
      The resting shrine
      Of Love Divine?

Hail ! Throne of Holy Trinity !
Thou ark of boundless charity !
O'er all infirm the canopy !
Peaceful shelter for all weary !
      Couch where lowly
      Find sleep holy !

Hail ! Jesus whom all adore,
Worthy of reverence evermore.
I come to Thee : Thine ear incline
As I draw nigh. With fire divine
      Inflame mine heart,
      And grace impart.

Give me a heart quite free from blame,
Contrite, filial, wrapt in love's flame ;
A will that though 'tis ever mine
Shall be transformed and made like Thine,
      Abundant flow
      Of grace bestow.

SAINT BERNARD'S PRAYER

O sweet Jesus, Shepherd Divine !
Sonship to God and Mary, Thine !
At the full fountain of Thine heart
Cleansing from sin do Thou impart.
       Father benign
       Thy love be mine.

Hail ! Splendour and Symbol Divine
Of Him whose glory is all Thine !
From the full treasury of Thy love
On those who plead to Thee above
       Thy gifts bestow
       With mercy's glow.

Lord Jesus Christ, within whose breast
Do dwell sweet peace and comfort blest,
May I, absolved from sin by Thee,
Ablaze with fire of charity,
       Ever abound
       With love profound.

Thy wisdom's depth doth us amaze.
Angels with harmony do Thee praise.
From Thee the truth divine doth flow,
As to John reclining ; may so
       I in Thee dwell
       Thy truth to tell.

TO CHRIST UPON THE CROSS

Hail! fountain of all goodness!
In Thee dwelleth all the fulness
Of the Deity bodily.
May the counsel Thou dost grant me
       Drive far from me
       All vanity.

True Temple of Divinity!
Bestow, I pray, mercy on me.
Thou who art of all good the shrine
Place me 'mongst those whose hearts are Thin
       O richest Shrine
       Of the Divine!

SAINT BERNARD'S PRAYER

VI. *Summi Regis cor, aveto.*

O Heart of Heaven's Eternal King!
With joyful heart Thy praise I sing.
Thee to embrace doth me delight,
And this wish doth mine heart incite
     With Thee to meet
     In converse sweet.

With what love hast Thou been conquered,
With what grief hast Thou been tortured,
That when suffering did Thee overthrow,
Thou shouldst Thyself on us bestow,
     And from death's sting
     Deliverance bring?

O how bitter was that death's deed!
O how ungentle, full of greed
That death which entered in the cell
In which the world's true life did dwell!
     O Heart most sweet,
     Such foe to meet!

By the death Thou didst undergo,
By the sufferings Thou for me didst know,
Heart beloved of mine heart, I pray
Mine heart in Thee may ever stay.
     It is my boast,
     I wish this most.

TO CHRIST UPON THE CROSS

O Heart beloved, aught else beyond,
Mine heart hath strayed, in wand'rings fond,
Hath been by world's vain things made hard.
Cleanse, soften, and let reverence guard
      This heart of mine,
      Again made Thine.

O may this heart of mine within,
Though it be full of guilt and sin,
With Thine own love be piercèd through,
That Thou mayst make it pure and new.
      Thus with love's pain
      Mine heart will gain.

Bloom forth and open wide, like flower
Whose fragrance far around doth shower.
Join to Thyself this heart of mine.
Purge, goad, and make it wholly Thine.
      Who Thee loveth
      Pain endureth.

Mine heart's living voice doth Thee greet,
Heart, full of love to me so sweet.
Do Thou to mine heart so incline
That Thy sweet love may be made mine,
      And mine to Thee
      Return from me.

277

SAINT BERNARD'S PRAYER

O let mine heart in Thy love keep ;
O let it not in torpor sleep.
From it may prayers and cries ascend ;
May they with adoration blend.
       May joy divine
       Be always mine.

O Heart of love, allied to Thee
In bonds of suffering may mine be ;
And, Jesus, Thy lot will be mine,
If this mine heart along with Thine
       Arrow of hate
       Doth perforate.

O mystic rose, in Thine heart-bower
Bloom forth, and let Thy fragrance shower ;
Expand Thy petals in heaven's light ;
Fill mine heart with longings bright,
       And with the fire
       Of pure desire.

O take mine heart within Thy breast,
That near to Thine it may rest,
And be in sorrow joyful most,
And when scarred, in Thy beauty boast.
       Let Thine Heart's thrill
       With love mine fill.

TO CHRIST UPON THE CROSS

VII. *Salve, caput cruentatum.*

Hail, sacred head, grazed and thorn-crowned,
Lashed, smarting, stained with blood around;
In disarray, yet with beauty still
That doth all loving watchers thrill,
  And rouseth songs
  From heavenly throngs!

All freshness with which life is deck'd,
All strength, have gone from Thine aspèct,
Yet while thus marred, thus racked with pain,
For me consenting to be slain,
  Me, a frail man
  Thy love doth scan.

In this Thy Passion, Shepherd Good,
Bestow on me the soul's true food:
The honey sweet, truth from above;
The milk, sweet too, the milk of love;
  Truth, from heaven sent!
  Love, transcendent!

My sinful self do not Thou spurn,
From me as worthless do not turn
With death now to Thee drawing near
To me Thine head incline, and here
  Clasped to my breast
  Find Thou brief rest.

279

SAINT BERNARD'S PRAYER

The sacred sufferings Thou dost bear
I should rejoice with Thee to share,
And on this Cross with Thee to die,
But, as I love Thy Cross, may I
   Beneath Thy Cross
   Meet this life's loss.

For Thy death, so full of shame,
Lord, I give thanks, and praise Thy name;
Thou, Love Divine, dost mercy shower;
O grant me that, at my last hour,
   Apart from Thee
   I may not be.

When I must lay me down in death,
O fail me not at my last breath;
In that solemn hour, I Thee pray,
Lord Jesus, come without delay;
   Look Thou on me
   And set me free.

O, when Thou biddest me depart,
Come for the welcome of mine heart.
Lover Divine, may Thine embrace
Receive my soul. O let me trace
   How on Thy Cross
   Was borne our loss.

LXVI. SAINT BERNARD ON WORLDLY VANITY.

I. *O miranda vanitas.*

O vanity that doth surprise so much excite !
  O love of wealth that causeth men such bitter
    woe !
O poison keen that doth with subtle serpent's bite
  Frenzy arouse for what doth pass as flaming
    tow !

Man, so wretched, think thou how death re-
    straineth all.
  Who hath there been from first who death hath
    not obeyed ?
No one doth know when will come to him death's
    call.
  Who to-day liveth, to-morrow from life may
    fade.

Why doth the world fight for glory that's vain
  For glory that never knoweth stability ?
As quickly doth that glory glide, as quickly wane,
  As potter's bowl, sure only of fragility.

SAINT BERNARD

Trust thou more in promises carved in melting ice
    Than in vain delusions that crumble into dust.
Misleading in rewards, its virtue only hidden vice,
    This world never hath welcomed days of loving
        trust.

Tell me, where is Solomon, once as king so wise?
    Or where is Samson, leader so valiant in strife?
Or Absalom, so fair, so attractive in guise?
    Or sweet Jonathan, lovely and pleasant in life?

Whither hath gone Caesar, so beyond others'
    reach?
    Or Dives the splendid, who sumptuously fared?
Tell me, where is Cicero, eloquent in speech?
    Or Aristotle, thinker, who most thought hath
    stirred?

So many brilliant leaders of the ages past,
    So many a face that once scanned a wide-
    spread realm,
So many a prince whose great kingdom did not
    last,—
    In the twinkling of an eye, death each doth
    o'erwhelm.

ON WORLDLY VANITY

*　　　*　　　*

O food of worms ! O mass of dust ! O glistening
  dew
  Of vanishing vanity ! Why wilt thou thyself
Extol, thine heart not knowing if to-morrow view
  Thee not ? In life seek others' good, not
  rusting pelf.

Fleshly glory in which the foolish glamour find
  In Holy Writ is likened to the flower of grass.
As tender leaf is whirled away by rapid wind
  So man's life from light of day is ordained to
  pass.

Naught thou mayst have to lose, do thou as thine
  own prize.
  What the world giveth, away it meaneth to
  snatch.
Think on things above; let thine heart dwell in
  the skies.
  Happy he who from the world can his love
  detach.

II. *Dic, homo, cur abuteris.*

Why dost thou life's gifts abuse?
Why dost thou not life rightly use?
Why desertest thou wisdom's way?
Why dost store loss for future day?
Why dost choose ease, and not soul's gain?
Do not thou yield to fear of pain.
Why to salvation's hope not cling
And to highest joys upward spring?

What availeth this world's glory?
Why dost heed its guileful story?
Many a sign thou dost see
That bewitched art thou knowingly.
The world from right doth glide aside
And with its gliding thou dost glide,
Following the transitory
Not what doth world's onward story
Enrich; seeing not its glory.

O vanity of vanities!
O cares that are inanities!
O why is dignity so sought?
Why is wealth heaped with so much thought?

The love of Christ, how it is wide!
How patiently for us He doth bide!
Christ's great goodness never faileth!
His compassion never fadeth!

284

LXVII. SAINT BERNARD'S DEATH.

[1153......62.]

Saint Bernard's life on earth came to a close on the 20th of August, A.D. 1153. Thus only sixty-two years had passed since he was born in his father's castle at Fontaines-les-Dijon. No more than forty-two years had gone by since he made the choice which opened out for him his marvellous career of mingled contemplation and activity, and led him to his strenuous life within monastic walls and in the outer world, in which he became the spiritual guide not only to his monks, but to all thoughtful minds in Western Christendom, and the counsellor too of rulers ecclesiastical and secular, in matters affecting the welfare of the Church and the conduct of their lives as bishops or kings.

Two and a half years previously the Abbot of St Denys, to whom he had shortly before written "I have loved thee from the very first, and shall love thee onwards unceasingly," had passed on to the life of the spiritual world.

A year afterwards Count Theobald of Champagne, the saint's lifelong friend and supporter, had been withdrawn from earthly activities.

Only a month before the Saint's own dear disciple and namesake—who for eight years had been Pope Eugenius III.—had been called away from the control of the Church on earth to the Church in the unseen world.

When his last illness came upon him, Saint Bernard rapidly faded away. When he had been but for a short time ill, his cousin Godfrey, the Bishop of Langres, and once prior of Clairvaux, came to him for counsel : but the feeble Abbot could not give heed to Godfrey's words. He was only able to say : "Do not marvel; I am now no longer of this world."

As his monks surrounded him, they tried to put away from their minds the despairing thought that they were to lose their spiritual father, and as it were entreated him to remain with them : "Wilt thou not have pity on this monastery, father? Wilt thou not have compassion on those whom thou hast hitherto cherished with consoling love ?" He himself weeping turned towards them as they wept, and lifting up to heaven his dove-like eyes, said that he was in a strait between two desires, to tarry with them, or to depart ; but he would submit to the divine will. In submission to that will he almost at once closed his eyes to open them no more. "Happy was the transit from toil to consolation, from expectation to reward, from conflict to triumph, from death to life, from faith to certain knowledge, from pilgrimage to the fatherland, from the world to the Father."

INDEX.

Abelard, xiv

Adam of S. Victor, vi

Alberic, 11, 12

Alberone, Archbishop of Trèves, 119

Aletta, Saint Bernard's Mother, xii

Alexander of Fountains, 109

Andrew, Saint Bernard's Uncle, 139, 182

Anselm, Saint, xi

Apulia, 84

Aquitaine, 235

Armagh, 159

Auxerre, Bishop of, 179

Baldwin, Brother, 85

Baldwin, King, 139

Bernard of Pisa, 221

Bonneval, Abbot of, 114

Bordeaux, Bishop of, 39

Bruno, Brother, 85, 129

Chalons, Church of, 11

Chartreuse, 5

Châtillon-sur-Seine, xiii

Citeaux, xii, xiii, xiv

Clairvaux, xiii, xiv, 8

Cluny, 1

Cluny, Abbot of, 152

Conrad II., xi

Chrysogonus, a Bishop, 85

Dijon, xiii, 172

Eugenius III., xi, 146, 221, 225, 237, 248, 285

Florence, 234

Fontaines-les-Dijon, xi, xiii, 285

Fulk, King, 139

Gaufridus, Bishop of Carnotes, 235

Geneva, Count of, 45

Geoffrey, Bishop, 18

Gerard, Brother, 85

Godfrey, Bishop of Langres, 286

Henry, Abbot of Fountains, 109, 112

Henry I., xi

Henry V., xi

Hugo, Count of Champagne, 8

Hugo de Bèse, 172

Humbeline, Saint Bernard's Sister, xii

287

INDEX

Innocent II., xi
Ireland, 159
Ivo, Master, 85

Langres, xiii, 116, 117
Louis VII., xi, 18
Luke, a Bishop, 85
Lyon, 118

Martin, Cardinal Presbyter, 234
Matthew, Bishop, 21
Melisendis, Queen, 139, 182
Melrose, 162
Metz, 121

Olric, Canon of Langres, 116

Pisa, 234
Poitiers, Count of, 41
Pontigny, 16

Rievaulx, 111
Robert, Dean of Langres, 116

St Anastasius, Abbey of, 132, 144

St Denys, Abbey of, 174, 175, 285
Sens, xiv
Sophia, Maiden, 57
Stephen (of Auxerre), 179, 180
Stephen Harding, xii, 13
Stephen, King, xi

Tescelin, Saint Bernard's Father, xi, xii
Theobald, Count of Champagne, 285
Toul, 120, 121
Troyes, Council of, 21

Valle-Clara, 111, 112
Valley of Light, xiii
Valley of Wormwood, xiii
Verdun, 120
Viterbo, 107

Wallen, Prior of Kirkham, 162

York, 162

This Index is supplementary to the "Contents," on pages vii, viii, ix, x.

For EU product safety concerns, contact us at Calle de José Abascal, 56–1°, 28003 Madrid, Spain or eugpsr@cambridge.org.

 www.ingramcontent.com/pod-product-compliance
Ingram Content Group UK Ltd.
Pitfield, Milton Keynes, MK11 3LW, UK
UKHW012329130625
459647UK00009B/170